T0355253

Political Corruption

Political Corruption

The Internal Enemy
of Public Institutions

EMANUELA CEVA
MARIA PAOLA FERRETTI

OXFORD
UNIVERSITY PRESS

OXFORD
UNIVERSITY PRESS

Oxford University Press is a department of the University of Oxford. It furthers
the University's objective of excellence in research, scholarship, and education
by publishing worldwide. Oxford is a registered trade mark of Oxford University
Press in the UK and certain other countries.

Published in the United States of America by Oxford University Press
198 Madison Avenue, New York, NY 10016, United States of America.

Library of Congress Cataloging-in-Publication Data
Names: Ceva, Emanuela, author. | Ferretti, Maria Paola, author.
Title: Political corruption : the internal enemy of public institutions /
Emanuela Ceva and Maria Paola Ferretti.
Description: New York , NY : Oxford University Press, 2021. |
Includes bibliographical references and index.
Identifiers: LCCN 2020058619 (print) | LCCN 2020058620 (ebook) |
ISBN 9780197567869 (hardback) | ISBN 9780197567883 (epub)
Subjects: LCSH: Political corruption. | Political ethics. |
Public administration—Moral and ethical aspects.
Classification: LCC JF1081 .C38 2021 (print) | LCC JF1081 (ebook) |
DDC 172/.2—dc23
LC record available at https://lccn.loc.gov/2020058619
LC ebook record available at https://lccn.loc.gov/2020058620

DOI: 10.1093/oso/9780197567869.001.0001

1 3 5 7 9 8 6 4 2

Printed by Sheridan Books, Inc., United States of America

Contents

Acknowledgments

Many have asked what it is like to write a philosophy book with four hands. In our experience, it has been a great adventure; talking through rough thoughts, exchanging drafts all over Europe and beyond, struggling with revisions, trashing entire chapters, reformulating, and redrafting. Throughout the process, no single paragraph was completed until we were both satisfied with it. We made this roller-coaster run smoothly perhaps because we have traveled the same academic path, even if we walked it with a small time lag. We began studying philosophy at Pavia, where Salvatore Veca introduced a whole generation of Italian students to analytical political philosophy, and Ian Carter encouraged them to pursue their studies in the United Kingdom. We were first at York and then at Manchester, where Hillel Steiner's acumen helped us survive the strenuous times of our PhD research. We are indebted to Salvatore, Ian, and Hillel in many ways, but perhaps the greatest debt we owe them is in showing us the importance of letting our own interests guide our research, rather than participating in the fashionable debates of the discipline.

So, we were not discouraged when we first presented our ideas on the inherent wrongness of political corruption and encountered some resistance. It is quite obvious, many told us, that political corruption is wrong: It has so many harmful consequences! Why, we were asked, would we bother investigating its nature any further? Over the past six years, we have managed to persuade some of those colleagues that the project was worthwhile. Indeed, we have found many philosophers and theorists willing to engage with us in discussions, as well as journals willing to publish the preliminary results of our research.

We have presented parts of this book in different venues. The present version has benefited greatly from the comments and discussions with the audiences of many events, including the ECPR General Conference, University of Hamburg (2018); the Royal Institute of Philosophy Public Lecture at the Department of Philosophy, University of Kent (2017); the Joint Sessions of the Aristotelian Society and Mind Association, University of Warwick (2015); and the Society for Applied Philosophy Conference, St. Anne's College, Oxford (2014). The workshop on political corruption organized at the Edmond J. Safra Center for Ethics of Harvard University (2018) gave us valuable insights provided by exchanges with Eric Beerbohm, Candice Delmas, Jenny Mansbridge, Tim Scanlon, and Dennis Thompson. In spring 2017, David Schmidz organized the Liberty Fund Conference "Freedom from Corruption" at Hermosa Beach, California, where we refined our ideas during challenging conversations with Adrian Blau, John Hasnas, Mark Knights, Elijah Millgram, Michael Munger, and Daniel Weinstock. We are also very grateful for the opportunity many philosophy and politics departments offered us to discuss our work in their seminar series, in particular the Blavatnik School of Government, Oxford (2019); University of Pavia (2016 and 2019); Université Paris I, Sorbonne (2018); University of Tel Aviv (2018); King's College London (2018); University of Bayreuth (2018); TU Delft (2016); Sciences Po, Paris (2015); Université de Montréal (2015); University of Trento (2015); and TU Darmstadt (2015).

In December 2018, we held a book manuscript workshop at the University of Pavia, which proved incredibly valuable in improving our work. In particular, Gillian Brock, Elizabeth David-Barrett, Antony Duff, Nik Kirby, Mark Knights, and Robert Sparling offered most helpful responses to the various book chapters. We are grateful to them and to the other participants, in particular to Michele Bocchiola and Sandra Marshall, for reading and commenting on the entire manuscript. We also owe a great debt of gratitude to the following scholars and friends, who have provided insightful comments on the manuscript at different stages of the writing process: Chiara Cordelli, Lisa Herzog, Mark Knights, Larry Lessig, Dennis Thompson, and Petr Urban. Many friends and colleagues generously provided various forms of assistance and encouragement in developing the ideas presented in this book. It is impossible to name all of them, but we particularly wish to mention Carla Bagnoli, Riccardo Ceva, Francesco Chiesa, Harry David, Rainer Forst, Andrea Fracasso, Anna Elisabetta Galeotti, Sigall Horovitz, Ina Kubbe, Miranda Loli, David Miller, Darrel Moellendorf, Dorota Mokrosinska, Nicoletta Parisi, Andrei Poama, Lubomira Radoilska, Daniele Santoro, Veith Selk, Kevin Valier, Alice Pinheiro Walla, Greg Whitfield, Jo Wolff, Lea Ypi, Bernardo Zacka, and Federico Zuolo.

For institutional support, Emanuela is indebted to the Edmond J. Safra Center for Ethics, Harvard University; Centre de Recherche en Étique, Université de Montréal; Blavatnik School of Government, University of Oxford; and her new academic home, the School of Social Sciences of the University of Geneva. Our participation in many conferences and the organization of seminars and workshops would not have been possible without the generous financial support of the Fulbright Commission (which awarded a research scholarship in philosophy to Emanuela in 2018) and the Cariplo Foundation and Regione Lombardia, which sponsored the project La corruzione delle relazioni (2018–2019). Maria Paola acknowledges her support received at TU Darmstadt and at the Research Centre "Normative Orders" at the Goethe University of Frankfurt am Main, and the Strategic partnership framework between Tel Aviv University and Goethe University of Frankfurt (2018), which made possible numerous profitable exchanges with colleagues in Tel Aviv. During our teaching seminars at the University of Pavia, the University of Genève, TU Darmstadt, and Goethe University of Frankfurt am Main, our students have been wonderful interlocutors and have helped us clarify many arguments we present in this book, making them more accessible to our audience.

Some chapters in this book draw on and develop arguments that we first advanced in articles published over the past couple of years. In particular, re-elaborations of some materials first presented in E. Ceva, "Political Corruption as a Relational Injustice," *Social Philosophy and Policy*, 35(2), 2019: 118–37 appear in Chapters 1 and 3. Some of the arguments defended in E. Ceva and M. P. Ferretti, "Political Corruption, Individual Behaviour, and the Quality of Institutions," *Politics, Philosophy & Economics*, 17(2), 2018: 216–31 are referenced in Chapters 1, 2, and 3, while there is some overlap between E. Ceva and M. P. Ferretti, "Political Corruption," *Philosophy Compass*, 2017, e12461 and Chapter 1. Some embryonic ideas expressed in E. Ceva and M. P. Ferretti, "Liberal Democratic Institutions and the Damages of Political Corruption," *Les ateliers de l'éthique/ The Ethics Forum*, 9(1), 2014: 126–45 have now been developed and are included in Chapter 3. The anticorruption strategy articulated in Chapter 5 shares some insights embryonically presented in E. Ceva and M. P. Ferretti, "The Ethics of Anti-Corruption Policies," in *The Routledge Handbook of Ethics and Public Policy*, edited by A. Lever and A. Poama (New York, Routledge, 2018): 255–266. Finally, Chapters 2 and 4 were developed from materials in M. P. Ferretti, "A Taxonomy of Institutional Corruption," *Social Philosophy and Policy*, 35(2), 2019: 242–63. We are grateful to the publishers and to the anonymous reviewers whose criticisms have motivated us to refine our work further until its present form.

We are most indebted to our editor at Oxford University Press, Lucy Randall, who believed in this project since the early stages and has assisted us through a winding but worthwhile review process. Hannah Doyle was a real star in guiding us through the entire process of book production. Working in such an amazing team of women was a truly rewarding experience by itself.

The fruitful exchanges with all of these people in various institutional venues have reinforced our conviction that our work can only be accomplished in an interrelated way with other people we meet in those contexts. But a project of this kind also requires the support of a more personal network of relationships as a valuable source of stimulus and encouragement. Also from this perspective, we have contracted many debts that we wish to acknowledge. This book was finalized during a complicated phase of Emanuela's life, characterized by a reappraisal of her deepest personal relationships. Therefore, throughout this process, maintaining the necessary concentration for this book was not easy. Thanks, for various reasons, go to Chiara, Elisabetta, Mary, and to Emanuela's family, Mariangela, Gian Luigi, Riccardo, Vittorio, Andrea, the unfailing companion of an intellectual and romantic life, and Daniela. It is to Daniela, to her spark of life so resilient and tenacious, that Emanuela dedicates this book. For their unfailing support, Maria Paola would like to thank her parents, Mariangela Ferrari and Enrico Ferretti, and her husband, Jens Steffek, whose intellectual curiosity and enthusiasm have proved invaluable motivation. Her daughters, Iolanda and Anita, are incredibly proud of this book, which is dedicated to them with unbounded love.

Introduction

In 2017, Ivanka Trump joined her husband, Jared Kushner, as a diplomat and an unpaid advisor to her father, Donald J. Trump, the president of the United States of America. The White House hastened to specify that Ms. Trump's emerging political role was voluntary work being performed "for the good of the country" (Oppenheim 2017; see also Keneally and Santucci 2017). Pressed by CNN, Jason Miller, the chief spokesperson for Mr. Trump's presidential campaign, forcefully denied any association of Ms. Trump's appointment with nepotism. What sense should we make of this case? Should Ivanka Trump's appointment be contested as wrong, and if so, based on what standards?

In this book, we argue that cases like the appointment of Ivanka Trump and her husband as White House advisors instantiate a form of political corruption whose wrongness can be best understood as a violation of a public ethics of office accountability. To understand how this case is a wrongful instance of political corruption (like many other forms of favoritism or clientelism), we must look at the features of the uses of powers of office by those who hold a role within public institutions. This means that we may not limit our analysis and assessment to the negative economic or sociopolitical *consequences* of the case by questioning whether, say, Ms. Trump was qualified for the job and her appointment could actually promote "the good of the country." We should not even limit our discussion to establish whether the appointment broke any federal *law* concerning nepotism, as that may not be the case because no paychecks were issued to Ivanka Trump's benefit. In fact, what

Political Corruption. Emanuela Ceva and Maria Paola Ferretti, Oxford University Press (2021). © Oxford University Press. DOI: 10.1093/oso/9780197567869.003.0001

matters first and foremost, from this perspective of public ethics, is the net of relations constituted by Ms. Trump's access to an office headed by her father and in which her husband also plays a major role. So, we should focus on the structure of uses of powers of office implied in this appointment. As we gain a better grasp of this net of relations, we can come to understand how political corruption works and is inherently objectionable as an internal enemy nested in the embodied structural relations between institutional roles.

This understanding of political corruption cuts across a wide range of occurrences of institutional malpractice or individual misconduct, including—as we shall see throughout the book—bribery, clientelism, embezzlement, state capture, and, of course, nepotism. By virtue of this encompassing nature, it overcomes the dichotomy between two mainstream views of political corruption. Some views focus on the "bad apples." These views conceive of political corruption as a personal vice, a trait of a person's character, or the misconduct of individual officeholders in breach of some rule of office for private gain. Other views concentrate instead on the quality of the barrel, pointing at processes that compromise institutional mechanisms. We challenge this dichotomy on the grounds that it is too brisk in treating institutional mechanisms as separable from the conduct of individual officeholders in their institutional capacity. This separation is at the basis of the programmatic suggestion that political corruption should be primarily tackled by addressing design flaws in the architecture of institutional mechanisms. This standpoint is questionable because it fails to reckon with what an institution is: a structure of interrelated rule-governed embodied roles to which powers are entrusted to perform specific functions. To recognize this defining image of an institution means to see that institutional mechanisms are not separable from the conduct of the occupants of institutional roles. And to see this feature means to be able to appreciate that the conduct of any one officeholder may change the interrelated action of an entire system of officeholders and, therefore, the institution's performance of its functions.

To be sure, we share the institutionalist intuition that we cannot reduce the corruption of institutional practices to the corrupt character of the specific persons who happen to occupy some institutional role, nor should we focus exclusively on individual cases of rule breaking, such as bribery. But we also think that we cannot understand the corruption of an institutional practice independently of looking at the interrelated actions of those who hold an office within that institution as they exercise their powers of office. From this point of view, to revisit the alleged case of nepotism from which we started, what makes it relevant as a wrongful instance of political corruption is not the Trumps' personal qualities, nor is the formal mechanism that regulated the appointments in question. Political corruption is, rather, nested in the web of institutional actions that the appointment constitutes. What matters is the failure to justify the rationale of the agendas thereby pursued by virtue of use of a power of office.

By concentrating on political corruption as a property of the interrelated actions of officeholders in their institutional capacity, we can study it as a matter of a public (not just personal) ethics of office in its own right. Our characterization of political corruption as a matter of public ethics is not intended to serve as yet another diagnostic tool to monitor and perhaps sanction the officeholders' conduct from the outside, or even as a standard of moralized behavior with which they should comply. Instead, framing political corruption in the context of a public ethics of office shifts the responsibility onto the officeholders. Officeholders are called, as a group of interrelated agents, to take responsibility for their conduct in their institutional capacity and for the functioning of their institution, as well as to engage in a critical and self-reflexive way with their conduct and its rationale. Especially when illegal actions are not clearly implicated (as in the earlier-mentioned Trump case), we want to stress the importance of developing tools and procedures that can support officeholders in a critical effort to reflect on their conduct in the interrelated exercise of their powers of office.

Adopting the perspective of a public ethics of office accountability aims precisely at this kind of critical exercise of self-criticism and guidance for institutional action. Likewise, anticorruption can be seen as an internal institutional practice that guides the institutional action of officeholders in nonideal conditions. Anticorruption, therefore, cannot be seen as merely one of many remedial policies whose implementation must be left to the contingent outcomes of cost-benefit analyses. Nor can it be seen as a matter of codifying certain external standards of conduct. From our proposed perspective, anticorruption is a self-reflective practice aimed at opposing political corruption from within an institution.

To see why the change of perspective we propose matters, consider the following scenario. A job vacancy opens up in the administrative department of a municipality. Sophia, the head of that department, is entrusted with the power to select a person to fill the vacancy. As it happens, Sophia had previously lent Mark some money, and Mark has agreed that, if he gets the job, he will use part of his salary each month to pay back his debt to Sophia. Mark applies for the vacancy, and Sophia eventually hires him.

This scenario intuitively speaks the language of political corruption—that is, the corruption of a *polis*, or of the rules that should govern the public order. Sophia is an officeholder who abuses the power entrusted to her public role as a means of promoting her personal interest (Philp 1997). What is more, to the extent that Sophia prefers Mark to other, better-qualified applicants, clearly her action is morally and quite likely legally questionable. Sophia has a corrupt motive: She uses her entrusted power to pursue a surreptitious quid pro quo. She acts in a way that is damaging for the collectivity (Mark is not the best candidate) and is contrary to the hiring regulation, which standardly commands impartiality of judgment.

As the Trump case illustrates, however, the circumstances in which an officeholder acts are rarely as clear-cut as those that frame the exchange between Sophia and Mark. Sometimes it is difficult to identify a direct beneficiary of an officeholder's action, especially when an officeholder uses her power of office not to promote someone's identifiable interest but instead, say, a certain political cause. This latter could be the case if Sophia had hired Mark on the basis of her knowledge that Mark shares her environmentalist political convictions. In other instances, the motive driving an officeholder's conduct might not be either self-interested or vicious at all. This could be the case if Sophia hired Mark because he is the needy breadwinner of a large family or the member of some historically marginalized minority group. The identification of what uses of a power of office are corrupt is thus far from immediate, as these hypothetical cases as well as the Trump case show.

Whatever forms it takes, political corruption is generally presumed to be a "disease" of the public order (Amundsen 1999), something that is negative for the society in which it occurs. It is much less well defined, however, as to what exactly makes political corruption wrong. Obviously, in a plain sense, political corruption is wrong qua unlawful when it involves formal rule breaking (e.g., in the case of such standard offenses as bribery and embezzlement). A further common position is consequentialist and identifies the wrongness of corruption as a function of the negative costs it produces (e.g., clientelism may cause inefficiencies in the provision of public services [Rose-Ackerman 1975], impoverish the population [Transparency International 2016], and undermine citizens' trust in public institutions [Miller 2017]). Other approaches employ corruption to indicate a very broad range of institutional pathologies associated with this term in the common language, such as plutocracy (Brock 2018). Finally, some institutionalists identify political corruption with mechanisms that cause institutions to deviate from their proper purposes (Lessig 2018).

Making sense of the wrongness of political corruption with reference to these approaches leads, however, to some serious uncertainties. To start, the normative evaluation of political corruption that some of these approaches deliver is too erratic. Not every instance of political corruption entails obviously unlawful action. Reconsider on this point the Trump example as a disputable break of the nepotism law. Think also of the much-debated case of private electoral-campaign financing, which is regulated by law in countries such as the United States. Moreover, it is apparent that many instances of political corruption have no clear and sizable costs or, in fact, they may bring about some advantages that arguably outweigh their costs. Bribes, for example, are sometimes considered as a "grease" to overcome the hurdles that may discourage foreign investments in developing countries burdened by a cumbersome bureaucracy. We should add that some of the current approaches tend to identify political corruption with democratic deficits in institutions or indeed with any instance of institutional failure. The risk is that too broad a use of the label *political corruption* loses not only conceptual rigor, but also practical relevance in identifying specific problems and possible solutions.

To salvage the conceptual specificity and practical relevance of political corruption, we must clarify how we should understand this phenomenon and why exactly it is wrong. To explain why, reconsider the situation of Sophia and Mark. We have said that, on an immediate reading, we can plausibly call Sophia's conduct corrupt and consider it wrong because she has favored Mark over other, better-qualified applicants with a view to recovering her credit. But what if Sophia's reasons were not self-interested (e.g., she only wanted to help needy Mark) or, in fact, were motivated by concerns of justice (e.g., she wanted to compensate marginalized Mark)? Also, what if, her original agenda granted, Mark was just as qualified as any of the other candidates? Were that the case, we could not either characterize or evaluate Sophia's conduct by looking at its damaging consequences. But imagine further that selection day was Sophia's lucky day and no other candidate showed up for the interview. Sophia's conduct could thus look formally impeccable, but can we safely say that she could therefore sleep tight, free of fears that she had acted in a wrongful manner?

Some readers may give an affirmative answer to this question. Instead, we devote the book to showing why we should resist this conclusion in this and other similar scenarios as that implicated by the Trump case. We pursue this endeavor by developing an encompassing but well-defined account of political corruption as an internal enemy of public institutions and by offering a cogent but nuanced assessment of its inherent wrongness from the perspective of a public ethics of office. The former task is essential to identify analytically the common root that makes political corruption a property of institutional practices as well as of the conduct of institutional role occupants (Ceva and Ferretti 2017) and distinguish it from other forms of institutional failure or malfunctioning. The latter task is crucial in any attempt to identify the normative core of the wrongness of political corruption even when some of its instances happen not to entail any lawbreaking or obvious socioeconomic cost (Ceva 2019).

To attend to the first task, we lay out in the first part of the book an analytical account of political corruption as a form of unaccountable use of an entrusted power of office. Officeholders make corrupt use of their powers of office when their action in their institutional capacity is sustained by an agenda whose rationale may not be vindicated as coherent with the terms of that power mandate. In this sense, corrupt officeholders are not in the position to give an account of their conduct as being coherent with their institutional role. This interpretation reveals the common root of many manifestations of political corruption that have so far sat quite uncomfortably together in the debate (e.g., bribery, clientelism, nepotism, embezzlement, and patronage). It also helps us to make sense of such cases as those in our examples. The reason why Sophia's conduct can be consistently characterized as corrupt across all the variations above is that recovering a personal credit is certainly not among the terms of the mandate with which the power of selection was entrusted to Sophia's office, nor is fulfilling some philanthropic commitment. Analogously, the power of appointing the president's advisors hardly encompasses the goal of corroborating family relations and cashing out the imports of the related personal connections. Moreover, while it is clear that officeholders do (and, as we argue in the book, should) enjoy margins of discretion and act in good conscience, it is not their call to establish unilaterally what justice or the "good of the nation" require (in general and in circumstances of moral disagreement in particular) and realize it through their idiosyncratic (albeit possibly well-advised) action.

In the second part of the book, we offer an assessment of political corruption as a relational kind of wrong that consists in the interactive injustice (Ceva 2016) of violating the officeholders' primary duty of office accountability. To see what this duty is and why it matters, we start from the basic view of an institution as a system of interrelated roles, occupied by human persons, to which powers are entrusted with a mandate. When officeholders act in their institutional capacity, they exercise a power that they possess only because they occupy a certain institutional role. The establishment of an institution thus creates a normative order within which officeholders acquire a special set of moral rights and duties that are mutually binding on them. Because institutional roles are structurally interrelated, any officeholder's capacity to act on her rights and duties depends on the other officeholders' performance of their respective rights and duties (Ferretti 2018). This structural condition makes officeholders fundamentally accountable to each other as concerns justifying the uses they make of their powers of office. To wit, solely through their institutional membership, people acquire a special moral duty of *office accountability*—that is, the duty of pursuing an agenda whose rationale may be vindicated as coherent with the terms of their mandate. Seen in this light, Sophia's duty as an officeholder is not just a retrospective obligation to answer for the outcome of the exercise of her power of appointment. Sophia has the prospective duty to engage in a justificatory practice of her conduct that demands that she is always in the position of showing how her institutional action falls within the boundaries of her power mandate—which is likely to command, inter alia, that considerations concerning her personal relation to Mark be excluded from the reasoning that guides her exercise of power. Because Sophia's action, as an instance of political corruption, fails this duty, she is not in the position to vindicate the rationale of her decision as appropriate. Thus, by her action she fails her primary duty of office and, ipso facto, alters the normative order of interactions within which her action occurs. This makes Sophia's use of her power of office inherently unjust as it constitutes dynamics of interaction that fall short of the requirements of office accountability. The same logic can sustain the assessment of Ivanka Trump's appointment as an advisor to her father as a wrongful instance of nepotism.

The division of our undertaking into these two tasks, analytical and normative, allows us to formulate complex descriptions of political corruption and make nuanced assessment of its wrongness. One of the interesting features of debating corruption is that this term is normally used with a pejorative connotation; when we call something "corrupt," we immediately think that it is an object of condemnation. But this understanding might be a source of confusion when, for example, the consequences of political corruption are not obviously negative (as we have discussed in our elaborations of Sophia's and Mark's quid pro quo), or when powers of office are used in a certain unorthodox way against an unjust or illegitimate institutional background (think of a Nazi official who withheld documents that could cause the deportation of Jews, or a police officer who fabricates evidence to convict a known pedophile).

Considerations of this kind have motivated some scholars to adopt very narrow definitions of political corruption to indicate exclusively abuses of public power for private gain (Philp 1997). The limitation of this narrow view is that it cannot account for many phenomena that belong to the semantic area of political corruption (e.g., patronage or state capture) but lack this public-versus-private dimension. Other commentators have thematized the tension between conflicting judgments on certain cases of corruption by developing the sui generis category of "noble cause corruption," which occurs when abusing the powers of office has positive consequences (Miller 2017). The problem with this solution, as we see it, is that it is limited to a consequentialist reading of political corruption and its wrongness, and therefore it cannot say much about the evaluation of those cases of political corruption whose consequences are not immediately visible, clearly measurable, or an object of contested evaluation.

We recognize the appeal of considering the immediately negative connotation of political corruption. In fact, this thought has prompted in part our own study in this book. It is an important thought because it brings out the need to clarify and investigate the criteria in virtue of which something can be considered corrupt and be condemned as such. Our two-tasked study tracks and pursues these two needs. As already explained, from our perspective, we can say that political corruption occurs whenever an office-holder, acting in his institutional capacity, uses his power of office to pursue an agenda whose rationale may not be vindicated as coherent with the terms of his mandate. This description applies to Sophia's hiring of Mark to recover her credit, Ivanka Trump's appointment as an advisor to her father, the Nazi official's withholding documents to avoid the deportation of Jews, or the police officer's fabricating evidence to convict a pedophile. Our study can make sense of the common core that qualifies these conducts as species of the same genus, thus doing justice to the internal complexity of this multifaceted phenomenon.

From an evaluative perspective, to say that political corruption is an interactive injustice suggests that there is always *one* sense in which it is inherently wrong. This sense refers to the disruption of the normative order of just interactions within just or legitimate institutional settings. However, to focus on this dimension of justice also allows conceding that sometimes certain instances of political corruption may be justified or, at any rate, excused. So, our normative analysis can establish the sense in which Sophia's use of her hiring power as well as the appointment of Ivanka Trump are corrupt and pro tanto wrong because of the unjust relationships dynamics constituted between Sophia, Mark, and her fellow coworkers, on the one hand, and between father, daughter, and son-in-law, as well as with the other members of the Trump administration, on the other. We can also say that in some cases the currency of interactive injustice is *insufficient* to condemn an act of political corruption, all things considered; the wrongness of certain acts could, in fact, be partially excused or entirely discounted. These are cases in which some pro tanto instance of interactive injustice preserves its inherent wrongness, but it can be excused, all things considered, in view of some other pressing judgment of end-state justice, as in the case of the deceptive police officer. Even more importantly, there are cases in which a prima facie interactive injustice can be fully justified, perhaps because it occurs against an unjust or illegitimate institutional background. In cases such as that of the deviating Nazi official, it would in fact be fundamentally flawed to speak of just institutional relations in the first place.

A peculiar feature of political corruption also emerges in this way: In certain nonideal circumstances, political corruption can have an important heuristic function because it brings to light deeper forms of structural injustices or illegitimacy that require questioning the very rules that govern institutions and their constitutive roles. In this sense, the corrupt behavior of an officeholder who bypasses the rules for the assignment of housing benefits in order to favor the members of a marginalized minority can be read as an act of resistance to the historic injustice of discriminating against these persons in social and political interactions. Our study thus allows making sense of a *moral remainder*, implicated in the occurrence of political corruption, as it emerges from the example we offered. Accordingly, we can develop nuanced evaluations of the wrongness of political corruption across heterogeneous circumstances, without thereby making the idea of political corruption collapse on that of the general injustice or illegitimacy of the institutions themselves. In this sense, the idea of political corruption as an internal enemy of public institutions indicates the discrete structural challenge that this phenomenon poses to public institutions, irrespective of their other qualities and even when they are well designed.

This normative view of political corruption offers the ground for developing by contrast three positive and far-reaching pursuits. First, our view of the relationally wrongful nature of political corruption is the basis for a positive account of an interactively just institutional system, centered on an ideal of *office accountability*, as the opposite of political corruption. The idea of office accountability is more precise and flexible than other contemporary alternatives based, for example, on institutional integrity. Institutions and power mandates evolve over time; while *integrity* suggests some rigidity and resistance to changes, we will show that *accountability* is dialogical, as it qualifies a justificatory practice articulated through relationship dynamics requiring someone who demands an account and someone else who has to give that account. The duty of office accountability is communicative because it qualifies the exchanges between the occupants of interrelated institutional roles. Through these exchanges, officeholders are called to engage in justificatory practices through which they can reciprocally call each other to respond for the ways in which they interpret their roles and the power mandates associated with them. The constant engagement in such justificatory practices makes the officeholders' interpretations of their roles and power mandates always open to revision and contestation.

Second, the view of political corruption as the opposite of office accountability lays the foundations for practices of institutional *answerability*, which is the way in which instances of political corruption are detected and retrospective and prospective individual and institutional responsibilities for political corruption are assigned (Ferretti 2019). These practices of answerability are necessary for upholding the normative order of just interactions between officeholders. They involve, for example, a careful analysis of institutional mechanisms and procedures to identify the structural weaknesses that, in virtue of their interrelatedness, may open the way to political corruption. For example, in the case of a politician who pays special attention to the needs of a pharmaceutical company that has contributed to her electoral campaign, our approach demands that we look primarily at the structural institutional relations within whose framework the politician acts in her interrelatedness with the other occupants of institutional roles. In other words, in order to understand possible sources of political corruption, we must look primarily at how the structure of interrelated institutional roles functions. We must do that to see, for instance, whether the institution is organized in such a way as to protect those officeholders who are especially exposed to powerful external agents known to push for the promotion of their interests. As a typical example, we have the lobbies of the pharmaceutical industry. Moreover, we should ask whether appropriate structures for conveying information about various forms of institutional wrongdoing are in place and whether their use is incentivized (e.g., through well-regulated channels for internal or external whistleblowing; see Ceva and Bocchiola 2018).

Third, looking at political corruption through the lenses of interactive justice helps us to bring into focus officeholders' new *anticorruption* obligations when political corruption actually occurs. We argue that officeholders are called, through their interrelated work, to respond to the inherent injustice of political corruption by restoring the normative order of office accountability that political corruption constitutively disrupts. This consideration prompts the recognition that anticorruption requires a complex set of proactive initiatives on the part of officeholders, as an institution.

We develop our public-ethics-based study of political corruption in five consecutive steps. The first two chapters of the book are devoted to analysis of the concept of political corruption, with a view to bringing out its inherently relational (neither exclusively individual nor institutional) dimension as a property of structures of interrelated embodied rule-governed roles.

In Chapter 1, we define political corruption as a form of unaccountable use of entrusted power. This definition consists of two conditions: There must be an officeholder who (1) acts in her institutional capacity (*office condition*) (2) for the pursuit of an agenda whose rationale may not be vindicated as coherent with the terms of the power mandate assigned to her role (*mandate condition*). We show that this definition of political corruption meets two important desiderata. First, it has the *explanatory* potential of revealing the many faces of political corruption in a way that is analytically accurate and able to do justice to the most common usages of this label. Second, it has the *discriminatory* potential of singling out the specificity of political corruption in a way that avoids redundancy with respect to other forms of political misbehavior or institutional malpractice.

In Chapter 2, we focus on current *institutionalist* positions that interpret political corruption as a primary dysfunction of some institutional mechanism. We agree that this position responds to an important practical need to move away from the practice of *finger-pointing* in corruption scandals and to redirect attention to institutional structures and practices. But we reject its *discontinuist* premise for which *institutional corruption* is a concept separate from that of *individual corruption*. We lay out a continuist view: In virtue of the interrelatedness of institutional roles, institutional corruption can always (and only) be understood by spelling out the relations between individual corrupt actions and institutional features. On this basis, we present a taxonomy that distinguishes between a *summative*, a *morphological*, and a *systemic* model of political corruption in institutional practices. By clarifying the structure of different corrupt institutional practices, we submit that these three models are effective diagnostic tools to identify different relational structures of political corruption and distinguish them from their effects.

The two following chapters are devoted to a normative discussion of political corruption and aim to pinpoint its wrongness as a form of interactive injustice, which consists in a violation of the officeholders' primary duty of office accountability. In Chapter 3, we explain how the focus on political corruption as a property of institutional structures of interrelated roles makes the relational aspect of the wrongness of political corruption emerge. To offer this explanation, we concentrate on the duty of office accountability as an institutional duty of interactive justice. Political corruption is a failure to act on this duty because it consists in an exercise of powers of office following an agenda whose rationale may not be vindicated as coherent with the terms of those power mandates. Therefore, corrupt uses of those powers fail the test of office accountability. They thus constitute an alteration of the normative order of interactions within an institution and, as such, are unjust. We show that political corruption retains this moral wrongness as a practice, independently of whether any of its specific instances imply unlawful action or produce economic, political, or social costs. We conclude the chapter by showing the advantages of our proposed office-accountability-based normative understanding of political corruption by contrasting it with recent impartiality- and integrity-based accounts.

In Chapter 4, we explain how the focus on the structural-interrelational features of political corruption (not only its consequences) allows for fine-grained attributions of individual and institutional responsibility for corruption and anticorruption

through practices of answerability. Drawing on our tripartite taxonomy of political corruption, we formulate differentiated ways of
assigning individual and institutional responsibility across different
instances of political corruption, and we propose to look primarily
at the "interrelated responsibility" that officeholders share for the
corruption of their institutional action. We show that while certain
instances require singling out corrupt agents and holding them li-
able to punishment for their wrongful behavior, in other cases it
makes better sense to attribute the responsibility for political corruption to a whole institution because of the specific patterns of
interrelation between its members and their roles. From this vantage point, we expound both retributive and restorative answers
to political corruption. The retributive answer includes punishing
corrupt officeholders and dismantling networks that support corruption. The restorative answer focuses on the division of roles, the
distribution of responsibilities, and the forms of control, incentives,
and rewards that can ensure that officeholders and institutions
stand clear of corruption in the future.

We close the book by presenting the pivots of an approach to anticorruption as a component of a public ethics of office accountability aimed at restoring an interactively just institutional setting.
In Chapter 5, we examine how understanding anticorruption as a
component of a public ethics of office accountability entails going
beyond standard regulatory or punitive approaches and developing good practices to supplement current strategies of institutional reform or to promote good governance standards. We thus
reorient anticorruption toward a commitment of public ethics
aimed at guiding officeholders' conduct as the occupants of institutional roles to oppose political corruption by restoring office accountability. The relational nature of anticorruption is consistent
with recognizing a generalized need for a change of institutional
culture that upholds the interrelated prospective responsibility of
institutional-role occupants. We show how this interrelatedness-
based approach has a primary importance relative to standard

practices of individualized finger-pointing or systemic institutional reform. Such a focus on interrelatedness is a necessary premise for realizing a public ethics of office accountability by establishing practices through which officeholders can help one another to use their powers of office in a way that ensures institutional well-functioning. These measures promise to uphold officeholders' interrelated responsibilities and sustain their public-ethical commitment to resist and counter political corruption.

Through this analytical and normative path, we aim to spell out three important conclusions from recasting the debate on political corruption in terms of public ethics. First, this recasting qualifies the judgments of political corruption. These judgments are based on an evaluation of institutional practices and individual officeholders' conduct, with a primary focus on the normative order of their role-based interactions. Therefore, these judgments are not primarily of the personal morality of the officeholders involved and their compliance with formal rules, nor can these judgments be limited to measurement of the economic, legal, political, and social costs caused by corrupt institutional dynamics.

Second, discussing political corruption as an object of public ethics helps to make progress on the attribution of responsibilities for corruption and anticorruption. Such responsibilities should be attributed to individual officeholders' *interrelated* ordinary work, rather than simply invoking either punitive actions for individual bad apples or a systemic intervention for general reforms concerning the very design of public institutions. This new approach helps to promote the realization of a structure of institutional relations that sustains office accountability as the positive opposite of political corruption.

Finally, by questioning the mainstream legalistic, punishment-based, and consequence-driven approach to anticorruption, we lay out new avenues for fostering an organizational culture of anticorruption. This level of action is necessary to discard the leniency that hampers identification of political corruption and, at the same time, to avoid instrumental uses of the language of corruption to single out any political villain or to condemn any dysfunctional institution. To see political corruption as an internal enemy means to identify it as a specific threat to public institutions and urge officeholders to act to defend those institutions from the inside.

1
What political corruption is

1. Introduction

In this chapter, we describe political corruption as a form of unaccountable use of entrusted power. We discuss the two individually necessary but jointly sufficient conditions for this form of corruption to occur: There must be a public official who (1) acts in her institutional capacity as an officeholder (*office condition*) (2) for the pursuit of an agenda whose rationale may not be vindicated as coherent with the terms of the mandate of her power of office (*mandate condition*).

The label *political corruption* has been used in heterogeneous ways in the academic debate as well as in the public discourse. Current uses of this label include references to bribes, misappropriations, acts of fraud, nepotism, and various forms of influence of private interests on political elections and governmental decisions (e.g., lobbying, state capture). In some cases, political corruption indicates the misconduct or particular vice of some officials; relevant officials are at times identified with public decision makers but may also include administrators and lower-level bureaucrats. In other cases, political corruption designates institutional malfunctioning. This mixed basket includes both instances of unlawful behavior (e.g., embezzlement) and legal but questionable institutional practices (e.g., the spoils system). Political corruption is sometimes taken to concern only those cases where someone uses her power of office to gain some personal material benefit (e.g., money or sexual favors); sometimes it describes uses of power that accrue to an official's political benefit by enhancing

Political Corruption. Emanuela Ceva and Maria Paola Ferretti, Oxford University Press (2021). © Oxford University Press. DOI: 10.1093/oso/9780197567869.003.0002

her influence (e.g., nepotism) as well as institutional practices that favor certain political factions or causes (e.g., private financing of electoral campaigns).

To complicate the picture, some attributions of "political corruption" that focus on the character of institutions are, in fact, figures of speech to indicate, inter alia, loss of integrity or decay of an institution. For example, one may lament that trade unions have lost their commitment to protecting workers' rights by taking up a broader political role that covers all manner of labor issues (including the conditions of those who are retired, unemployed, or still in school). So, one may say that the unions' mission is "corrupt" because unions have lost the sense of their original purpose and, therefore, they have lost sight of their "nature."

As a result of this multiplicity of usages, the attribution of political corruption has become very popular to indicate an ongoing suspicious activity within an institution, but these usages risk making the attribution of this label idle and uninformative. The many different usages of political corruption are philosophically disappointing because of the conceptual uncertainties they bring. But this heterogeneity also shows important practical difficulties with the identification of relevant instances of political corruption and of a clear target for anticorruption policies. For instance, we could ask whether anticorruption should focus primarily on large-scale proposals for institutional reform or, rather, on policies aimed at developing a civic sense that the corruption of public officials may not be tolerated, even if corrupt officials are isolated "bad apples." Surely our answer depends on how we conceptualize political corruption: whether primarily as a structural institutional phenomenon or as a matter of individual conduct.

A philosophical discussion of political corruption must, therefore, start with conceptual clarification. This clarificatory work must meet two desiderata. First, it must have the *explanatory* potential of distinguishing the many faces of political corruption in a way that is at once analytically accurate and able to do justice to

WHAT POLITICAL CORRUPTION IS   21

the most common usages of this label. Second, it must also have the *discriminatory* potential of singling out the specificity of political corruption in a way that avoids redundancy with respect to other forms of political misconduct or malpractice. A clarificatory work aimed at meeting these two desiderata is a precondition for any subsequent normative assessment of the phenomenon. We do this work in the first part of the book by characterizing political corruption in entirely descriptive terms.

We introduce a definition of political corruption that can be useful to identify possible instances of this phenomenon and distinguish it from other cases of controversial conduct by an office-holder or institutional practices. We do not say anything in this chapter (or in the next) about how a particular instance of political corruption is wrong; that normative discussion will be our task in the second part of the book. In what follows, we introduce the idea that political corruption is a deficit of office accountability, and we elaborate on the two conditions of its occurrence (§2). Then we show how these conditions substantiate an account of political corruption that is true to the internal complexity of this phenomenon (§3) but are also capable of isolating the particular use of a power of office that distinguishes it from other kinds of controversial uses (§4).

2. Political corruption as a deficit of office accountability

Simply stated, political corruption is the corruption of public officials and institutions. Taking the cue from a number of formulations of political corruption across various disciplines,[1] we propose that, to understand this form of corruption, we must look

---

[1] See, for example, Heywood (2015); Miller (2018); Philp (1997); Rose-Ackerman (1999).

into public institutions to analyze the uses of the power entrusted to the occupants of institutional roles, that is, the officeholders. Understanding this institutional background is essential to understand how political corruption is best interpreted as a form of unaccountable use of entrusted power.[2] In this context, the term *unaccountable* means "impossible to account for" rather than "not subject to accountability." To see what this means, we propose considering the following two components of a use of power that give substance to two individually necessary but jointly sufficient conditions for there to be a case of political corruption: There must be a public official who (1) acts in her institutional capacity as an officeholder (*office condition*)[3] (2) pursuing an agenda whose rationale may not be vindicated as coherent with the terms of the mandate of her power of office (*mandate condition*). The office condition regards the *agent* of political corruption, whereas the mandate condition concerns the *action*. The two conditions of political corruption are the negative image of the constitutive features of a well-functioning institution. In what follows in this chapter, we first describe what a well-functioning institution is (a topic we revisit and expand in Chapter 3) and then explain the two conditions of political corruption with reference to that description.

2.1 Office accountability and institutional functioning

Basically, an institution is a system of embodied rule-governed roles (the offices that human persons occupy) to which powers

---

[2] We introduced this idea in Ceva and Ferretti (2014) and developed it in Ceva and Ferretti (2017, 2018). With respect to these earlier works, we have dropped the term *surreptitious* to characterize a corrupt use of entrusted power in favor of the label *unaccountable*. This choice of terms more immediately pinpoints our concern with vindicating the uses of entrusted power and avoids possible confusion due to the resonance between "surreptitiousness" and "secrecy." We are grateful to Candice Delmas, Nikolas Kirby, and Dennis Thompson for their comments on this definitional point.

[3] This condition also features in Philp (1997, 2015).

are entrusted with a mandate. All roles in an institution are interrelated.[4] Institutions are defined by what their members do as an interrelated group of agents in virtue of the powers entrusted to the various institutional roles. The raison d'être of an institution comprises the normative ideals that motivate its establishment and, consequently, its internal structure and functioning. Different power mandates are entrusted to different institutional roles with a view to ensuring that the officeholders' interrelated work can make the institution function. Because institutional roles are so interrelated, the well-functioning of an institution structurally and necessarily depends on the ability of each and every officeholder to exercise their powers of office in keeping with the terms of that power mandate.

To be sure, an institution's raison d'être is neither internally monolithic nor diachronically static. One single institution may perform multiple functions at the same time, and their interpretation may evolve over time and space. As academics, for example, we are well aware that our institutions perform educational and research functions; sometimes these functions are even in tension with each other. Moreover, we are witnessing a growing bureaucratization of our institutions, to which increasing administrative functions are attached. These changes reveal an evolving understanding of the institutional raison d'être of universities and, relatedly, of the characterization of the mandate entrusted to us. The choice of speaking of an institution's functions—rather than, for example, its purpose (see Miller 2014)—suggests this generality and identifies a common conceptual ground that different conceptions of institutions (e.g., teleological, functionalist) can share.

These variations granted the establishment of an institution confers upon the officeholders a special normative status. In their

---

[4] For a classic presentation of an institution as a "pattern of roles," whereby roles are capacities "in which someone acts in relation to others," see Emmet (1966). For an overview, see Miller (2014).

institutional capacity, officeholders are endowed with a set of rights and duties that they can only exercise over each other by virtue of their status of officeholders. In order words, to establish an institution is to establish multilateral deontic relations between officeholders, who cannot engage in those relations absent or outside of that institutional context. Thus, when people act in their institutional capacity, they acquire ipso facto a status that comes with the power to do things to each other that they would not otherwise have the power to do as "bare agents."[5] So, if a random stranger knocks on my door and demands that I give her some money, she is a thief; but if this stranger is a tax collector, she has the right to demand that I give her money and I have the duty to give it to her.[6] Accordingly, entertaining institutional relations entails that a person has a general duty to abide by not only the law or the principles of *personal ethics* (such as the harm principle), but also the body of moral norms and other distinctive normative commitments (rights and duties) that are binding on an individual qua the member of that institution (the domain of *public ethics*).

The exercise of the officeholders' institutional rights and duties structurally depends on the conduct of others, so that a well-functioning institution is one in which all officeholders exercise their powers of office in pursuit of an agenda whose rationale may be vindicated as coherent with the letter (the governing rules) or the spirit (the rationale) of those powers mandates.[7] That officeholders pursue such an agenda by their action in their institutional capacity is crucial to ensure that their interrelated action

---

[5] In this sense, officeholders are "institutional entities"—that is, "an object with properties or characteristics that depend on the existence of an institution" (Guala 2016, XVII).

[6] Note that, with some qualifications, this characterization of an institution could also apply to the private sector insofar as we look at rule-governed organizations (e.g., a corporation). However, because this book discusses political corruption, we shall not tackle this possible extension and shall instead focus solely on public institutions.

[7] Ceva and Ferretti (2014), 130. This twofold connotation distinguishes our view of political corruption from what Warren (2004, 329ff.) has labeled (and criticized) as the "modern view," which only refers to the formal aspects of rule following.

makes the institution function—that is, to be faithful to its raison d'être, in view of which the various institutional roles have been established and powers entrusted to them with a mandate. Thus, a well-functioning institution that can maintain the normative order it establishes is structurally dependent on the officeholders' interrelated action. This means that the officeholders are fundamentally accountable to each other for the uses they make of their powers of office when they act in their institutional capacity. This is the idea of "office accountability."[8] Office accountability is the property of a well-functioning institution in which officeholders are in the position of giving each other an account of the rationale of the agenda that underpins the uses they make of their power of office and show its coherence with the terms of that power mandate.[9]

Office accountability governs the institutional relations between officeholders. As participants in these relations, officeholders are established with the authority to require that one another "gives an account" of their action. The core of this idea is relational because it links "those who owe an account and those to whom it is owed" (Bovens et al. 2014, 6). Because this idea is a basic component of a public ethics of office, it should work as an ex ante regulative constraint on what courses of action officeholders may or may not pursue in their institutional capacity. Office accountability is thus importantly different from and irreducible to the standard idea that officeholders are *answerable* ex post for the uses they have made of their entrusted powers. Of course, the idea of answerability is significant too, and we retain it as part of what it means for officeholders to be responsible for their conduct (see Chapter 4).[10] Nevertheless,

---

[8] For an earlier formulation, see Ceva (2019).

[9] Many commentators on institutional theory recognize the importance of justifying institutional action with reference to power mandates. For example, in the field of professional ethics, see Emmett (1966) and, in legal theory, see Winston (1999). For a broader discussion, see Applbaum (1999). For the Kantian interpretation of officeholders' action on mandates, see Ripstein (2009).

[10] Another idea that belongs to this semantic area is what H. L. A. Hart has called "role-responsibility," the idea that "whenever a person occupies a distinctive place or office in a social organization, to which specific duties are attached . . . , he is properly said

our idea of office accountability has an action-guiding aspiration that is irreducible to practices of answerability.

An important feature of office accountability is its mutuality.[11] Before administering an experimental drug to a patient, a physician ought to ensure that all risks are adequately considered and that the patient's consent has been sought. This procedure is necessary to establish whether administering that drug is in the patient's best interest (and it is not a response, say, to the connection the physician has established with the pharmaceutical company that produces that drug at the latest medical convention sponsored by that company). The physician should follow this course of action not just as a matter of abiding by whatever professional rule of conduct is legally enforced in the hospital where she works, nor is the physician required to act in that way only out of the moral and professional integrity she owes to the patient and to herself (in good conscience). By following this course of action, the physician is also in the position of justifying her conduct to her colleagues with reference to the terms of her power mandate, thus fulfilling office accountability. By her action, the physician is accountable not only to the other doctors who work on a team with her and are involved in the patient's care, but also to the hospital staff (the nurses, assistants, and administrators) whose performance depends on the physician acting on a rationale that may be vindicated as coherent with the terms of the power mandate defining her role. In this sense, while the professional duties of personal morality and professional ethics demarcate the boundaries of the physician's

---

to be responsible for the performance of these duties, or for doing what is necessary to fulfil them" (Hart 1968, 212). As our subsequent discussion will show, our idea of office accountability has a dialogical connotation that is extraneous to Hart's idea of role-responsibility. For a broader analysis of the inherent properties of structured forms of human interactions, see Ceva (2016).

[11] Notice that "mutuality" distinguishes our account of the power dynamics within an institution from a popular formulation of such dynamics in terms of a "principal–agent" relation. For a philosophical reading of corruption in terms of the principal–agent problem, see Sparling (2014).

individual conduct, she is also structurally accountable for the rationale of her conduct in her institutional capacity to her fellow hospital workers. These latter workers are equally accountable to her and, thus, share the same authority to insist that every officeholder acts according to a rationale that coheres with the terms of their power mandate (which certainly do not include basing medical decisions on pleasing a generous pharmaceutical company).

The mutuality of office accountability points out the relational nature of the power dynamics *within* an institutional setting. Of course, officeholders are *answerable* to external third-party enforcing authorities. For example, when an action is unlawful, an external authority will intervene for distributing punishments. Certainly, democratic institutions such as parliamentary assemblies must also respond to the public. However, we have explained an essential sense in which officeholders are fundamentally *accountable* to one another. This sense of accountability is characteristic of the institutional context in view and refers to the specificity of the powers of office. It is, therefore, irreducible to a general idea of *acceptability*, whereby an action is vindicated when it can be made acceptable to a general public on the ground of some shared reason (e.g., reasons of justice).[12]

---

[12] Notice that the exact composition of the community of mutually accountable members varies in consideration of the uses of power at stake and the kind of institution under scrutiny. For example, it may include the components of a commission of experts or it may extend to cover the citizenry at large when we consider a democratic governmental organization. These details should be assessed on a case-by-case basis. But it is clear that we do not refer (only) to accountability to superiors. For a discussion of various perspectives on accountability, see the articles in Bovens et al. (2014). A possible way to state the point is to say that the structural relations between officeholders are second-personal (see Darwall 2006; Feinberg 1970c). This jargon also suggests that this kind of mutual accountability could be dubbed, in Kantian terms, "publicity." This expression indicates that the terms of reference for justifying the uses officeholders make of their powers of office are a matter of "mutual" knowledge; they are something that all members of a community know and know that the others know too. David Luban has provided an insightful discussion of this interpretation of mutual knowledge with reference to Kant's principle of publicity in *Perpetual Peace*. This principle commands that for an action to be justified, it must be shown that its maxim is "compatible" with publicity (Luban 2012, 155, 170). The mutual character of this idea of accountability qualifies it as directed to all members of a relevant community of knowledge whose composition

2.2 Office accountability and the conditions of political corruption

We have thus far characterized office accountability as a property of the relations between officeholders, with specific reference to the terms of the mandate entrusted to their roles. The point we must emphasize now is that an institutional system informed by a public ethics of office accountability is the positive opposite of political corruption. In other words, when officeholders act in their institutional capacity (office condition) following an agenda whose rationale is unaccountable with reference to the terms of their power mandates (mandate condition), their conduct is corrupt.

A helpful illustration of the unaccountable nature of corrupt action comes from observing the typical operations of redescription through which corrupt officials try to account for their conduct. Typically, they describe bribes in the language of gifts or donations and translate their clientelist relations as instances of mutual trust. These operations of redescription are in fact a constant feature of political corruption throughout history. Recently, such operations have prominently involved Ivanka Trump's appointment as a diplomat and an advisor to her father, President Donald Trump. The White House officially described her emerging role as voluntary work "for the good of the country" (Oppenheim 2017), thus denying any association with nepotism and corruption. But history should have made us aware of such subterfuges.[13] A flagrant illustration comes from the diary of Samuel Pepys (1633–1703), a corrupt naval administrator during the late Stuart period in Britain. Pepys secured for himself a substantial number of payments

necessarily depends on the nature of the institution and the kinds of power exercised under scrutiny.

[13] For an insightful historical reconstruction of these operations of redescription in early modern Britain, see Knights (2018). In Chapter 4, we expound the implications of these, more or less intentional, operations for the possibility of assigning moral responsibility for corrupt actions. For a discussion of how occupying a professional role may change the description of an action, see Applbaum (1999, 77ff.).

from suppliers to the navy in exchange for his help in obtaining contracts, posts, or settlement of some accounts. While he carefully registered all of these entries in the diary, Pepys took pains to account for them as tokens of friendship and politeness or as acknowledgments for services rendered (see Knights 2014). The form that Pepys's redescriptions of his corrupt conduct took is quite interesting in itself: They are not part of a formal criminal defense, nor do they stand up to public scrutiny. Pepys wrote a diary, which mimicked the logic of making himself generally accountable for his institutional conduct. We think this is a telling suggestion of the position that office accountability (rather than a more standard idea of answerability) occupies the core of political corruption.[14]

Take note that for an institution to be accountable in our sense of the term, it does not necessarily have to be "transparent" (see O'Neill 2006). Some uses of powers of office may be transparent in the sense that they are made in the open. But even when an officeholder acts in the open, we can say that her use of power is unaccountable to the extent that the rationale of the agenda that she pursues in her institutional capacity may not withstand scrutiny as coherent with the terms of that power mandate. So, nothing in our view commits us to the refusal of any space for secrecy. For example, critical decisions about military operations are routinely made behind closed doors. However, this condition of secrecy does not necessarily entail that any unaccountable use of entrusted power is occurring behind those doors. Office accountability demands that those who are entrusted with the power to make those decisions do so in accordance with an agenda whose rationale may be vindicated as coherent with their power mandate. This agenda may include reasons of personal and national security, but it certainly excludes the promotion of partisan financial interests or attempts to divert

---

[14] For a discussion of self-deception and other forms of tainted reasoning through which officeholders try to rationalize their involvement in systemically corrupt practices, see Ceva and Radoilska (2018).

public opinion, say, regarding some national economic crisis. Independently of whether such uses of power are more or less transparent, those who make them must be capable of showing the coherence of the rationale of their agenda with the terms of their power mandate. This requirement applies to all officeholders, even if their having to answer for their conduct is an eventuality that might never occur. This thought is coherent with the idea that office accountability is a regulative idea;[15] it is thus meant to be a means of guiding officeholders' actions. In this sense, political corruption as a deficit of office accountability is a matter of public ethics for institutional roles.

This public ethics is relevant for all public institutions and applies in cases of both "grand" and "petty" corruption. Grand corruption indicates the behavior of politicians and institutional decision-making practices, whereas petty corruption involves the behavior of administrators, bureaucrats, and institutional practices of rule implementation (see Amundsen 1999, 3). Our characterization of political corruption regards both dimensions because the agents who act in either of these capacities are entrusted with powers of office that may be used in a relevantly similar corrupt manner (see Ceva and Ferretti 2014, 2018). So a public ethics of office accountability concerns not only the conduct of elected politicians, judges, and public administrators, but also that of workers in the public sector. For example, security officers should comply with health and safety protocols, and teachers in public schools should teach the national curriculum. In this light, we can see that political corruption may concern the conduct of public officeholders entrusted with the institutional power to make and implement laws and policies, and it may occur within strictly political institutions (e.g.,

---

[15] This interpretation tracks Luban's presentation of the function of Kant's principle of publicity "as a principle of first-person deliberation by decision-makers (rather) than as a principle of third-person evaluation by observers" (Luban 2012, 168).

a parliamentary commission in a democracy) as well as in public institutions such as state schools and hospitals.

Although exercising the powers of office is rule-governed, a measure of discretion is generally allowed concerning how precisely a particular officeholder may perform his tasks. The power mandate establishes, among other things, the areas and ways in which officeholders' discretion can be exerted. Discretion does not accrue only to those officeholders, like judges, whose job description includes the exercise of their judgment. It is a standard feature of institutional roles. So, for example, customs inspectors may ask any questions they consider necessary to verify suspicion of any particular traveler. The officeholders' leeway for discretion is among the reasons that inevitably make exercises of powers of office contestable. This means that both the interpretation of powers of office and their modes of exercise are predictably the object of disagreements. Discretion and disagreements in this context are arguably healthy: Would we really desire that officeholders make unreflective use of their power? Or that their actions be mechanically aligned to some algorithm? [16] These preferences are hardly plausible and quite uncommon. In fact, the most important implication of recognizing the endogenous contestability of institutional action is the need to develop a public ethics of office capable of guiding this action and making officeholders answerable for it.

Acknowledging these disagreements is a useful reminder that power mandates are not set in stone and beyond contestation (we revisit this notion later in this chapter and in Chapter 3). For example, the role of an administrator entrusted with the power to decide the allocation of housing subsidies allows for some discretion in making judgments concerning the eligibility of an applicant. The very criteria used to identify the most deserving applicants among equally eligible applicants are undoubtedly subject to many

---

[16] For a formulation of this challenge in terms of a contrast between "judgment" and "authority," see Applbaum (1992).

contrasting interpretations. Moreover, the content of a power mandate—not only its interpretation or its use—is a possible object of contestation and disagreement. The bureaucratic idea that officials should suspend their judgment entirely and honor their duties of office no matter what is hardly plausible. This idea has been frequently disputed, for example, with reference to the defenses offered by Nazi officials at the Nuremberg trials; during these trials, the defendants' notorious strategy was to reject responsibility on the ground that they had just acted according to the duties of their office (see Ehrenfreund 2007). Our mandate condition does not presuppose an unconditional obedience of this sort. It is, rather, compatible with some degree of role contestation. In certain cases, as discussed in Chapter 3, disobedience may occur within the framework of a more general contestation of the legitimacy of some specific institutional arrangements.

More generally, we can say that officeholders, in virtue of the discretion normally attached to their role, generally find themselves using their own judgment to decide how to implement their mandate concretely in specific instances. Clearly, even if they act in their institutional capacity, their judgment is likely to be influenced by their personal beliefs and convictions. However, because officeholders' conduct in their institutional capacity inevitably and structurally depends also on that of other officeholders, their judgments and conduct must be coherent with the terms of their power mandate in order for them to sustain by their interrelated action the well-functioning of their institution. Our conceptual analysis of political corruption thus identifies a public ethics of office that gives officeholders guidance to sustain the well-functioning of their institution by making any use of their powers of office (and of the discretion that goes with them) accountable.[17] In this context,

[17] The idea that officeholders use their discretion legitimately insofar as they act within the scope of their mandate is arguably at work in Kant's account of state acts. For a discussion of this issue, see Ripstein (2009).

the key to tackling political corruption is not the reduction of the discretionary aspects of office per se, nor is it a matter of eliminating the space for role contestation (e.g., see Anechiarico and Jacobs 1996; Philp 2001). The point is, rather, to restore officeholders' capacities to make an accountable use of those prerogatives of their office. We discuss this point extensively in Chapter 5.

In a well-functioning institution, the terms of officeholders' power mandates should be designed with clarity. This will verify that the boundaries of discretion and the issues over which it can be rightfully exerted are well circumscribed and justified, in keeping with an institution's raison d'être. So, for example, the question of whether single parents or large families are more deserving of housing benefits may not plausibly be left entirely to the sense of fairness of any one individual administrator. Rules of adjudication, which reflect the political and social priorities of the administration, must be established. However, the application of such rules to any specific case can presumably allow for some discretion to adapt, for instance, to such eventualities as a sudden divorce or the death of a family member. These objective institutional provisions granted, it is clear that officeholders are ultimately responsible for making their actions in their institutional capacity accountable and, thus, making their institution well-functioning. [18] There is no institution beyond the officeholders' interrelated actions. To pinpoint this idea is perhaps the most important analytical point we make in this section. It will be crucial both for investigating the relation between individual and institutional corruption in Chapter 2 and for presenting our idea of "interrelated responsibility" for corruption and anticorruption in Chapter 4.

Before we proceed with the argument that will pave the way for these discussions, a final important qualification is in order. This

---

[18] This conclusion echoes Applbaum's invitation for officials to stand on "their two feet" and make use of their judgment when they exercise their power of office with discretion (Applbaum 1992, 254, 272–73).

qualification concerns the immediate association that some readers might be tempted to make between our idea of office accountability and a democratic ethics, or the inference that a public ethics of office must be democratic to uphold accountability. We present our normative proposal for a public ethics of office accountability in Chapters 3, 4, and 5. For now, we can say that the idea of office accountability does not belong solely to a democratic public ethics; it applies to any public institution that meets our formal characterization. While our argument is compatible with a democratic reading, it is thus more general on two counts. First, by distinguishing *accountability* from *transparency*, it also covers those instances of political corruption that are not concealed but are done, rather, in the open (e.g., when it is a well-known practice that to trade goods in country X, one is expected to bribe customs officers).[19] Second, our argument so far has offered a *description* of political corruption without making any *normative* claim (based on democratic exclusion or otherwise) concerning why it is wrong.[20] What is important for now is to emphasize that, whether concealed or done in the open, absent office accountability, the uses an officeholder makes of her power of office are corrupt.

3. The many faces of political corruption

To cash out the clarificatory potential of our view of political corruption, we must pose two considerations. First, we need to explain how our view can make sense of the many faces of this

[19] For Warren, "corrupt democratic decisions and actions in a democracy are always covert" (Warren 2004, 333). For a discussion of the space of secrecy in democratic ethics, see Mokrosinska (2018).

[20] See, in contrast, Warren (2004, 330, 333–34). This general descriptive approach also sets our argument apart from impartiality-based accounts of political corruption (Kurer 2005; Rothstein and Varraich 2017). These accounts are at once normative and more specific. (The reasons why a certain use of entrusted power may not be vindicated might include the idea that it violates the impartiality of office, but this is not necessarily the case; see Ceva and Ferretti 2018 and Chapter 3.)

phenomenon. Second, we need to elucidate the idea that this extensiveness is not overinclusive, by discriminating what uses of powers of office are rightfully included under or excluded from the heading of political corruption. We attend to the first endeavor in this section; the second is the object of §4.

So, what uses of a power of office are corrupt? In §2, we saw that political corruption may involve uses of powers of office concerning either decision making (grand corruption) or rule implementation (petty corruption). In addition, it concerns cases in which the use of power is either unlawful (e.g., embezzlement) or lawful (e.g., nepotism) and cases that accrue either to the personal and material (e.g., bribery) or the political and nonmaterial (e.g., influence peddling) advantage of an officeholder.

Our concept of political corruption is inclusive with regard to the items that might figure in a corrupt officeholder's agenda. Unlike other, popular views of political corruption, we need not include only personal types of advantage that accrue to the officeholder's material benefit.[21] Our idea of political corruption also covers, for example, favoring the members of a specific interest group for an increase in political influence (as may be the case with clientelism; see also Thompson 2018). Furthermore, and perhaps less straightforwardly, we can also encompass actions aimed to promote a particular cause or support a person about which the corrupt officeholder has a powerful feeling. This may be the case with familism as illustrated by the appointment of Ivanka Trump and her husband, Jared Kushner, as advisors to the president. Admittedly, these latter kinds of use of public power are more difficult to pinpoint than those involving more obvious material private gains or quid pro quo (as in the case of bribery). Nevertheless, their elusiveness does not make them any less relevant insofar as they meet our two conditions of political corruption.

---

[21] See, in contrast, Rose-Ackerman (1999) and Philp (2015). See also Johnston (2005).

Moreover, our account of political corruption tracks uses of powers of office that might be either unlawful or lawful. So, it encompasses such epitomical instances of political corruption as bribery and embezzlement, which most legislation recognizes as criminal offenses. But consider also such highly contested practices as the Padrino system practiced in the Philippines, a form of political patronage through which anyone seeking to enter the country's political arena is customarily expected to earn political debts and dispense political favors to gain influence. While the various manifestations of this practice are not generally outlawed, they are frequently considered cases of political corruption. The many specific ways in which such aspects are formally regulated vary across the legal arrangements in force in specific contexts and different political and social cultures. Our analysis of political corruption provides a conceptual toolkit that cuts across such contextual differences. The capacity to track both lawful and unlawful corrupt acts is an entailment of the dual nature of the violation of an officeholder's power mandate we introduced in the previous section. Because corrupt uses of a power of office may violate the letter as well as the spirit of that power mandate, political corruption may involve a deficit of office accountability as concerns either some formal rule (e.g., the rule of access to some public services in cases of favoritism) or the rationale with which power is attributed to a particular role.

Consider, for example, the rules that govern access to such health services as abortion. In many countries across Europe (for instance, in Italy) where access to abortion services is legal and provided by the national health system, there is a conscience clause that allows physicians to refuse to perform such services on the grounds of their moral convictions.[22] However, the concession of such a legal exemption is subject to some rules of professional

---

[22] For the case of Italy, see the Law 194/1978, http://www.salute.gov.it/imgs/C_17_normativa_845_allegato.pdf.

conduct, which typically include obligations to refer patients to nonobjecting colleagues and to provide them, in any case, with either pre- or postabortion care. These conditions notwithstanding, many doctors have been reported as failing to comply with these obligations, thus making abortion services practically unavailable in some instances (see Ceva and Ferretti 2014). Now imagine that, within such a legal framework, Mario, a junior physician who works in a state hospital, refuses to perform abortions not out of his conscientious conviction but to please the chief surgeon, who is known to be a devout Catholic with an antiabortion agenda. Mario hopes that, in so doing, he will boost his career. Insofar as the law does not require physicians to declare the reasons for their appeal to the conscience clause, Mario does not violate any formal rule, and his conduct is therefore lawful. In our account, however, Mario is acting legally, but his conduct is corrupt. We can call his conduct corrupt because it is sustained by an agenda whose rationale may not be vindicated as coherent with the spirit of his power mandate. While the mandate of Mario's role includes the conscience clause, it certainly does not include the prerogative of making an instrumental use of it to promote, for example, his career.

Of course, recognizing these instances of political corruption from a third-personal perspective—by looking only at Mario's behavior—is no easy task and in cases of conscientious refusal may also be too invasive. Behavioral patterns might be observed (e.g., is Mario himself a member of any "pro-life" association?) and compensatory costs could be associated with the exemption (e.g., an increased availability on weekends). These provisions could offer consistency cross-checks and disincentives to free-ride or abuse the clause. However, they would only provide an indirect indicator of the rationale of the agenda that underpins Mario's conduct. In response to this point, we must reaffirm that the demands of accountability associated with exercising the powers of office should mainly work as a regulative idea that constrains the kind of uses of power in which an officeholder should embark in the first place.

Because our account of political corruption encompasses uses of powers of office that may be either lawful or unlawful, the demands of accountability associated with those uses are a matter of a public ethics of office rather than legal regulation for institutional roles. Political corruption may, therefore, occur even within well-designed institutions with meticulously regulated formal roles and practices. Political corruption is, in this sense, an internal enemy of public institutions.

4. Political corruption and other controversial uses of the power of office

We have just illustrated how our reference to deficits of office accountability is capable of tracking the distinguishing shared feature of many different instances that are commonly, but arguably unreflectively, considered under the heading of political corruption. While this illustration corroborates the extensiveness of the explanatory potential of our view, we must be careful that this quality does not bring with it a risk of overinclusiveness. This risk is serious because it would undermine the discriminatory potential of our view, thus failing the clarificatory ambitions that motivate our conceptual analysis. In this section, we show how the two conditions that articulate our definition of political corruption qualify our view as capable of living up to this clarificatory ambition. Be reminded that any given use of entrusted power is politically corrupt if there is a public official who (1) acts in her institutional capacity as an office-holder (office condition) (2) in order to pursue an agenda whose rationale may not be vindicated as coherent with the terms of the mandate of her power of office (mandate condition). These two conditions must be jointly satisfied to qualify a case as an instance of political corruption distinct from other instances of institutional malfunctioning or individual misconduct.

In fact, some uses of a power of office might be controversial because someone has acted out of incompetence or perhaps because certain institutional practices have been designed carelessly, either in good faith or for some harmful intent. As we show in this section, we might be tempted to classify some such cases as instances of political corruption. But, if our account holds, we would be misguided unless we can show that such uses of power refer to an action carried out (1) in someone's institutional (and not personal) capacity and (2) are items of an agenda whose rationale may not be vindicated as coherent with the terms of that power mandate. To show that our two-condition view is capable of discriminating between these cases helps avoid conceptual mishaps (which would be analytically and philosophically disappointing). Most importantly, it offers a perspective from which to call something "corrupt" is actually helpful in understanding a salient feature that makes it relevant for a moral and political normative assessment.

To illustrate, let us start with Lisa, a public official who is in charge of supervising projects for the promotion of wind-energy technologies. Suppose that Lisa uses the connections she has made with different kinds of energy providers through her job to seek funds to contribute to the campaign of a candidate whose political platform includes a plan for the development of nuclear plants. We could call Lisa hypocritical and question her moral integrity. But the relation between Lisa's institutional role and her personal conduct is incidental. Insofar as she acts in her personal capacity and free time, we cannot say Lisa's institutional conduct is corrupt, although the rationale of the agenda she pursues may not be vindicated as coherent with the mandate that should regulate her conduct when she acts in her institutional capacity.

Consider now the case of Mark, who holds this same position in another office and, as part of his job, must find contractors for locally implementing various wind-energy-related projects that his office is promoting. Suppose further that Mark signs a contract with an energy provider, which it turns out is investing part of its profits to support a subsidiary company engaged in developing nuclear energy. If Mark was not aware of this incident, perhaps because he failed to perform all necessary background checks before signing the contract, we could consider his conduct in his institutional capacity as careless and incompetent. However, absent an agenda whose rationale may not be vindicated as coherent with Mark's power mandate, we could not say that his conduct is corrupt, despite the appearances.

So, what would a case of political corruption look like? Consider Silvia, who has the institutional role of selecting experts for assessing the sustainability of the conversion to wind-energy technologies. Imagine now two possible scenarios. In the first scenario, Silvia receives a bribe from an energy provider that has invested in the development of nuclear power plants; in exchange for the bribe, she appoints an expert advisor who is known to have a nuclear-friendly attitude. In the second scenario, Silvia selects an expert advisor in exchange for a report that offers scientific evidence in support of the sustainability of nuclear energy against wind energy in line with her own position on the matter. In the first scenario, Silvia acts unlawfully (bribery is outlawed in many legislations) in exchange for a material personal gain (the bribe). The second scenario does not involve any formal lawbreaking (Silvia's office allows for some margins of discretion), but Silvia acts to push forward a particular, nuclear-friendly policy that reflects her own views. Both scenarios are instances of political corruption because they illustrate actions that Silvia performs in her institutional capacity as she pursues an agenda whose rationale may not be vindicated as coherent with, respectively, the letter and spirit of her power mandate. In the second scenario, one might well think that Silvia is genuinely persuaded that nuclear energy is a safe option, and her manipulation of the evidence might be the most effective way to put this conviction to use in the interest of what she thinks is the best institutional decision. However, by her action, Silvia takes for herself the role of the expert as she tries to steer the institutional decision through a power that is not in her mandate. In doing so, she makes herself unaccountable to the other officeholders and deprives them from the possibility of joining in assessing the evidence on which she has formed her own conviction, as her mandate requires. To call Silvia's conduct corrupt in both situations, we can thus pinpoint an unaccountable use of a power of office.

A further scenario to consider is one in which a public official acts in his institutional capacity but uses his power in a way that may not be vindicated as coherent with the terms of his mandate to promote a cause that he regards as just or, at any rate, morally worthwhile. Imagine, for example, the case of James, a public official who uses his power of office to sabotage the implementation of projects for the conversion to nuclear power. James is concerned that these projects would impose an unfair environmental and health risk on people in whose vicinity the nuclear plants will be built. Because the people in the neighborhood have only a modest political leverage on the decision concerning the conversions, James thinks that they would suffer an environmental injustice, unless his institution acted in a way that protected them. Say that James is in charge of filing scientific evidence on the sustainability of different kinds of energy sources, but he purposefully destroys any nuclear-friendly reports he receives, knowing that some of those reports speak to the economic advantages of nuclear energy, and those advantages could be balanced against the health and safety of the people in the neighborhood. These cases are frequently referred to as instances of "noble-cause corruption" (Miller 2017, 89 ff.).

What could we make of cases of "noble-cause corruption" within our conceptual framework? These are cases in which the office condition is satisfied. In our example, James—like Silvia—acts in his capacity as the officer responsible for filing scientific reports on the sustainability of energy policies. How about the mandate condition? To be sure, James's action of sabotage may not be vindicated as coherent with the letter of the mandate with which his power is entrusted to the role he occupies. But arguably James's conduct—unlike Silvia's—*could* be vindicated with reference to the spirit of the mandate, to the extent that the organization in which he works is outspokenly committed to protecting the health and safety of all citizens as a matter of priority. His action of sabotage could be the only way to protect the health and safety of the people in the neighborhood of the nuclear plant. To the extent that this case can be made, we could formally describe James's conduct as corrupt. However, we wish to suggest that calling James's conduct "corrupt" is not obviously helpful to clarify what salient feature of this case makes it the object of a political and moral assessment (more on this assessment in Chapter 3). Presumably, the rationale of James's agenda could be vindicated by appealing to general principles of justice inspired by considerations of fairness and the importance of someone's right to health. But when someone acts in violation of some rule in the name of justice or morality, we already have the philosophical categories to investigate this use of power; we can describe and assess it as an instance of conscientious rule breaking (e.g., in cases of civil disobedience) or legitimate role contestation.[23] A case for considering these instances under the rubric of political corruption could technically be made, consistently with current usages of "noble-cause corruption." However, we think such a case is not very helpful but redundant because such instances can fruitfully be discussed within an already-existing and consolidated conceptual and normative apparatus. In other words, what makes such cases salient is not so much a deficit of office accountability as their expressing a form of resistance to some injustice.

---

[23] For a discussion, see Applbaum (1992, 250 ff.) and, more generally, Applbaum (1999).

5. Conclusion

In reaction to the many conceptual uncertainties that derive from the polysemy of political corruption, we have devoted this chapter to an analysis of this idea as a kind of unaccountable use of the powers of office. Specifically, we have endeavored to vindicate both the explanatory and the discriminatory potential of this view.

On the one hand, our analysis has brought to light a unified concept of political corruption capable of making sense of the specific use of entrusted power that draws together different instances of this multifaceted phenomenon. These are uses of a power of office whereby the officeholder acts in her institutional capacity (office condition) but pursues an agenda whose rationale may not be vindicated as coherent with either the spirit or the letter of the mandate of her power of office (mandate condition). Taken together, these two conditions qualify political corruption as a deficit of office accountability. We have shown how this is a shared feature of cases of grand and petty corruption, which involve both lawful and unlawful individual actions or institutional practices and accrue to the personal and material as well as to the political and immaterial advantage of some officeholder. Each of these instances of political corruption has its specific connotation, but they all share a common root consisting in a particular use of powers of office. One substantial result of our conceptual analysis in this chapter is thus a characterization of political corruption capable of explaining many of its major manifestations as different tokens of one same kind. As we show in the next chapter, this explanation has significant implications for the tenability of the conceptual distinction between individual and institutional corruption as recently advocated in philosophical debate.

On the other hand, we have also shown how our unified conceptual framework is not at risk of being overinclusive. Indeed, we have vindicated the discriminatory potential of our view as it is capable of differentiating corrupt uses of powers of office from other instances of controversial individual conduct or institutional practices. In these latter cases, an officeholder acts to pursue a controversial agenda, which, however, fails to satisfy either the office condition (when an officeholder acts in her personal rather than institutional capacity) or the mandate condition (when an action is not part of an agenda whose rationale may be vindicated as coherent with an officeholder's power mandate). Our analysis also suggests that the salient features of some cases frequently addressed under the conceptual rubric of political corruption are best understood if interpreted with a different, more specific conceptual apparatus because the parlance of political corruption might in fact be confusing rather than helpful. These are cases of "noble-cause corruption," which we have suggested interpreting with the conceptual tools of conscientious rule breaking or role contestation. Our analysis has thus culminated in a characterization of the conceptual boundaries of political corruption capable of discriminating between different forms of controversial use of a power of office.

We have thus offered a characterization of what features make cases of political corruption salient for a normative assessment, in which, however, we are not yet ready to engage. Our intent in this part of the book is descriptive and analytical. In the next chapter, we extend this commitment to the question of how our unified conceptual framework can make sense of political corruption in both its individual and institutional manifestations.

2

Political corruption: individual or institutional?

1. Introduction

In Chapter 1, we defined political corruption as a deficit of office accountability. This definition centers on the officeholders' use of their powers of office, when they act in their institutional capacity, in the context of the interrelatedness of their institutional roles. We explained that when such powers of office are used for the pursuit of an agenda whose rationale may not be vindicated as coherent with the terms of the power mandate, an officeholder's conduct is unaccountable and therefore corrupt. The focus on office accountability as a regulative principle for the use of powers of office is crucial to understanding exactly which actions instantiate political corruption as a matter of *individual conduct*. The emphasis on officeholders' acting within a system of interrelated roles brings to the fore the patterns of institutional interaction that instantiate political corruption also as a matter of *institutional practice*. This chapter explores the relationship between these two aspects of political corruption.

Because of political corruption's double nature, our view of it reconciles the individual and institutional dimensions of this phenomenon by bringing to the fore their shared structural root, which lies in the officeholders' interrelated use of their powers of office. In this way, we indicate a way forward that bypasses the current dichotomy between individual and institutional corruption. This dichotomy is the central piece of many "institutionalist"

Political Corruption. Emanuela Ceva and Maria Paola Ferretti, Oxford University Press (2021). © Oxford University Press. DOI: 10.1093/oso/9780197567869.003.0003

positions, which interpret political corruption as a primary dysfunction of some institutional mechanism. The proponents of this institutionalist turn deem it necessary to go beyond what they view as a limited study of political corruption as a discrete problem of "bad apples" (or of public officials who abuse public power for private gain) who need to be isolated to eradicate this form of corruption. Instead, the proponents of this institutionalist view have argued that a much more pressing problem is that institutions themselves can be "bad barrels" (see Lessig 2013, 2014, 2018; Miller, Roberts and Spence 2005; Philp 2015; Thompson 1993, 1995, 2005). That is, institutions themselves often provide an environment that not only allows political corruption, but even creates incentives for it. When political corruption becomes entrenched in institutional mechanisms, it has a more profound political and social impact than individual action, and its negative consequences endure well beyond the time in which corrupt individuals remain in office. This institutionalist view of political corruption thus extends the range of relevant instances from the more conventional individual actions such as bribery to such elusive institutional practices as the private financing of electoral campaigns.

One reason for privileging this institutionalist perspective is to move away from the practice of "finger-pointing" and finding scapegoats in political corruption scandals. But some advocates of the "institutionalist turn"—Lawrence Lessig (2018) and Dennis Thompson (2018) in particular—have gone further and have offered a theoretical defense of *institutional corruption* as a concept separate from that of *individual corruption*. In this institutionalist view, corrupt practices appear to benefit an institution, while they also undermine or incapacitate its ability to fulfill its purposes. These authors emphasize the link between corrupt institutional rules and mechanisms and the impaired functioning of an institution. We illustrate and discuss this institutionalist approach in §2.

Although we recognize that political corruption has a two-fold dimension (individual and institutional), we challenge one core idea of these institutionalists: the conceptual separateness of individual and institutional corruption. This idea has led its proponents to drive a wedge between these two dimensions of political corruption, thus failing to recognize their common root and origin (see, e.g., Rodwin 2013; Marks 2013). At the core of this idea of separateness is the thesis of the "discontinuity" between corruption as a matter of individual behavior and as the feature of an institution. In its stronger version, defended, for example, by Lessig (2018), the discontinuity thesis implies that institutions may be corrupt even when none of their members are. Challenging this view in §3, we defend a "continuity" thesis. This thesis explains how institutional corruption can always and only be understood by spelling out the structural relations between the features of an individual's corrupt conduct and those of some institutional mechanisms.[1]

It is necessary to reject the institutionalists' discontinuity thesis because it treats institutional mechanisms as separable from individual officeholders' conduct and suggests that political corruption should be primarily tackled by addressing design flaws in the architecture of institutions (Thompson 2018; Lessig 2018; Weinstock 2019). We regard this separation as descriptively unwarranted because it fails to recognize what an institution is: a structure of *interrelated*, rule-governed, *embodied* roles to which powers are entrusted to perform specific functions. To say that institutional roles are embodied means that it is not possible to view institutional mechanisms as separate from the action of the occupants of those roles, the officeholders. And to say that institutional roles are interrelated means that any officeholder's action

---

[1] The continuity thesis was introduced in Ferretti (2019). Miller (2017) defends a more restrictive view of a continuity approach by identifying some forms of individual corruption as amenable, via causal links, to the corruption of institutions.

may change the performance of (some of) the others' institutional roles and, therefore, the institution's performance of its functions (thus failing what we have called its raison d'être). While our analysis takes seriously the institutional environment in which political corruption occurs, we think an institutionalist approach that focuses on the quality of the "barrel" as separate from that of the "apples" inside it cannot give an appropriate account of the institutional mechanisms through which political corruption occurs. As discussed in Chapter 4, a number of concurrent normative considerations favor adopting the continuity thesis. These considerations refer mainly to possible solutions for assigning and distributing responsibility for political corruption. For the time being, suffice it to say that the continuity thesis helps us to make sense of the possible relations between the individual and the institutional dimensions of political corruption. To spell out these two dimensions is critical to doing justice to the relational nature of the exercise of powers of office in keeping with the defining structural features of public institutions.

Exploring the relationship between the different dimensions of political corruption, in §4 we develop a taxonomy that distinguishes between a *summative*, a *morphological*, and a *systemic* model of political corruption as it concerns institutional practices. We argue that any possible corrupt institutional practice falls within one of these three models. Moreover, by helping us to make sense of the structure of different corrupt institutional practices, the three models are effective diagnostic tools to identify different relational patterns of political corruption and distinguish them from their effects.

In §5, we discuss an illustrative case of systemic corruption to offer a closer observation of the dynamics and relations of this particularly intricate phenomenon. We conclude, in §6, with some remarks on the general applicability of our taxonomy to the structural analysis of cases of political corruption.

2. Institutionalist explanations of political corruption

For the institutionalists, individual corruption occurs when an officeholder obtains personal gain in exchange for promoting someone's personal interests. A corrupt character or a corrupt motive is an essential element of this form of political corruption (Lessig 2018, 12, 19; Thompson 1995). An obvious example is bribery, where the officeholder's behavior or judgment is influenced by the prospect of receiving a personal and material gain. Of course, officeholders may legitimately seek personal gain from public office, for example, through their salary or through enhanced career prospects. Therefore, not all personal gains of office are problematic, or at least not problematic in the sense of being corrupt (see Stark 1997). There are gains that exceed or violate the general and agreed rules of compensation and can motivate individual corrupt conduct. Such gains are certainly relevant as a breach of personal morality or professional ethics and may consist, for example, of money, gifts, or sexual favors. However, not all cases of individual corruption are also significant at an institutional level. For the institutionalists, an officeholder's individual corrupt behavior is also politically (and not only personally) problematic when it is systematic and widespread so as to cause general damage to an institution by affecting its dynamics.[2]

Most importantly, for the proponents of the position under scrutiny, institutions may be corrupt in deeper and subtler senses than when they are populated by corrupt individuals. While the proponents of this view defend quite diverse approaches and

---

[2] Note that the model of institutional corruption is not characteristic of just political institutions. Churches and sports associations are also vulnerable to institutional corruption. However, the preoccupation with political institutions is prominent in the current philosophical literature. See, for example, the epitomic case of private electoral campaign financing (Thompson 1995; Lessig 2003, 2018) or the case concerning the influence of the pharmaceutical industry on policy making (Lessig 2013, 2018; Rodwin 2013).

employ diverse methodologies to identify political corruption in institutional practices, we have isolated three recurrent and prominent explanations of institutional corruption: *teleological*, *substrate*, and *separateness* explanations.

The teleological explanation revolves around an institution's ability to fulfill its purposes. Seumas Miller (2017, 81), for one, holds that institutional corruption occurs where corrupt behavior undermines institutional processes or institutional purposes. Focusing on corruption as impairing institutions in serving their defining *ends*, Miller offers a teleological explanation of institutional corruption. He identifies the cause of institutional corruption as individual behavior that impacts institutions. In this way, Miller recognizes a *causal continuity* between the individual corrupt behavior of some officeholders and the corruption of institutional practices that are thus negatively affected. He does not drive either a conceptual or a practical wedge between the individual and the institutional dimensions of this phenomenon. However, he also insists that by focusing on institutional practices, we can appreciate a set of very serious political and societal damages that are much larger than those deriving from individual instances of corrupt behavior that do not have wide consequence for how institutions may achieve the purposes they are designed to serve.

There is another version of the teleological explanation that points at institutions as *structured* in such a way that makes them unable to serve their essential purpose. Larry Lessig (2011, 2014, 2018) is the most prominent advocate of this approach, which is also defended in some of Dennis Thompson's early writings (see Thompson 1995). This formulation of the teleological explanation of institutional corruption purports to flesh out how we can have politically relevant forms of corruption even in the absence of individual unlawful or otherwise-questionable behavior. For Lessig and (the early) Thompson, the cause of institutional corruption is not necessarily an individual corrupt action; instead, political corruption may be nested in institutional structural mechanisms.

These are cases of what Miller (2017, 73) dubs "institutional corrosion" to emphasize the absence of an individual source of political corruption. Thompson and Lessig, however, find "institutional corruption" a useful category of its own, for it refocuses the attention on structural dynamics of political corruption, whose study should take priority over the (sometimes vain) task of establishing continuity links between the institutional and individual manifestations of this phenomenon.

The paradigmatic illustration of a corrupt institutional practice—one that both Thompson and Lessig have discussed at length—is the private financing of electoral campaigns. In the United States, candidates who run for public office may receive financial support from diverse private sources. The practice of attracting sponsors is not only legal, but also crucial for all politicians aspiring to be elected, and, in this sense, it is vital for democratic practice. Individual small donations for a candidate may reveal supporters' political preferences. However, at the same time, a small group of wealthy elites has arisen, who make large political contributions with the goal of influencing election outcomes and policy making (Barber, Canes-Wrone, and Thrower 2017, 271–88). So it may happen that, once elected, a member of Congress—who has received financial support from, say, a private company—pushes some regulation that aims at reducing the fiscal pressure in the area in which that company operates. He does so in order to ensure future financing for his campaigns, which in turn may pave the way to reelection. In this sense, for these institutionalists, we cannot say that the congressman has a corrupt character; his actions are not motivated by a corrupt personal motive, and his behavior does not entail any violation of the rules. Nevertheless, from the perspective under scrutiny, this is an instance of institutional corruption in the political sphere because, by responding to the interests of large donors, members of Congress impair the capacity of this institution to fulfill its defining purpose, which is to be the expression of government "for the people." Notice that it is not the practice of private donations per se that makes Congress corrupt; rather, it is the practice of large donations and the donors' ensuing political influence that distort the democratic process. Thompson and Lessig thus call "institutional corruption" a form of democratic deficit instantiated in private electoral campaign financing to indicate the degeneration of a practice that was originally intended to promote the interest-based representation of all groups in society.

A further consideration is in order. As Lessig (2014, 2018) explains, people regard as corrupt the very practice of campaign financing, and not the candidates who seek sponsors. This mindset is understandable for Lessig because candidates do not seek money for personal gain (as in cases of bribery), but rather because it is the institutional practice of campaign financing that by its very nature demands that candidates seek large donations to be successful in the elections.[3]

This consideration brings us to a second explanation of how an institution can be corrupt independently of the character of its members: It can provide favorable circumstances for political corruption. This is what we call the substrate explanation of political corruption in institutional practices. It is apparent that some institutional mechanisms may provide the terrain for individual corrupt behavior to flourish, either by creating incentives for political corruption or by making political corruption the price one must pay to be part of the system.[4] In the earlier example, given the terms of the electoral competition, candidates are incentivized

---

[3] Lessig (2011, 7) explains the urgency of considering corruption in terms of improper political influence rather than focusing on individual corrupt action as follows: "The great threat to our republic today is not from the hidden bribery of the Gilded Age, when cash was secreted among members of Congress to buy privilege and secure wealth. The great threat today is in plain sight. It is the economy of influence now transparent to all, which has normalised the process that draws our democracy from the will of the people."

[4] Weinstock (2019) argues, for example, that democratic systems, being organized in an adversarial manner, are more exposed than other regimes to political corruption because they are designed to attract competitive characters. As an effect, not only during the electoral competition, but also in the legislative phase, partisanship tends to prevail in a way that may undermine the democratic goal of attending impartially to the interests of all citizens.

to seek private financing for their campaigns on pain of not being elected. Following this explanation, the causal continuity between a corrupt institution and the corrupt behavior of some officeholder within it is reversed compared to the teleological explanation; institutional practices may cause individual officeholders to act corruptly. In the institutionalists' explanation, however, this causal nexus does not necessarily entail that the congressman of our example is himself a corrupt person because he does not act out of a corrupt motive. Instead, his actions are totally understandable in virtue of the mechanisms by which he got into power. What should be questioned for institutionalists is, rather, the mechanisms that incentivize those actions.

The teleological and the substrate explanations of institutional corruption recognize a causal relation between the institutional and the individual dimensions of this phenomenon. In the teleological account, institutional corruption may arise from some individual corrupt behavior sustained by an individual corrupt motive, such as personal gain, or a vice, such as greed. In the substrate account, however, political corruption has an institutional origin, but it manifests itself through individual action. Thompson (2018) holds that neither of these explanations can capture the most salient aspects of institutional corruption. He argues, instead, that institutional corruption must be considered a separate concept from individual corruption. Unlike individual corruption, institutional corruption is typically characterized by the absence of individual corrupt motives or, in other words, by the absence of a personal commitment to promoting interests exogenous to the purposes of an institution. In paradigmatic cases of institutional corruption, such as that of private electoral campaign financing, candidates and donors may be motivated to benefit the institutions (e.g., by contributing to the democratic process). However, Thompson emphasizes that, in the system within which they operate, they unavoidably undermine the institutions' mechanisms and general architecture (i.e., when candidates serve the donors' interests instead of those "of the people"). In this way, institutional corruption is a property of the very practices of the institution in which it is embedded and takes the form of what Montesquieu called "the disease of the political body" (Thompson 2018, 3). This is what we call the *separateness explanation* of institutional corruption.

To a certain extent, we share the widespread idea that institutional practices should be the primary unit of study of political corruption. However, Thompson's version of the institutionalist position is stronger, and it claims that institutional corruption is an altogether separate phenomenon from the corruption of individual officials. Central to the separateness explanation of institutional corruption is the emphasis on the discontinuity between the concepts of individual corruption and institutional corruption: One concept is neither reducible nor amenable to the other.

To summarize, the family of institutionalist approaches to political corruption is heterogeneous. However, we have identified three main explanations of what institutional corruption is. According to the *teleological explanation*, one can recognize institutional corruption from the fact that institutions are incapacitated to serve their ends. The focus is on the damages that individual corrupt behavior causes to institutions. The second explanation, the *substrate explanation*, points at the institutional practices and mechanisms that create conditions favorable to establishing corrupt behaviors. Both the teleological and substrate explanations admit a *causal link of continuity* between individual and institutional corruption. The third explanation, the *separateness explanation*, conceives of institutional corruption as a separate concept (in discontinuity with individual corruption) in which the very practices embedded in an institution, while intended to serve the institution, end up also corrupting it by undermining its mechanisms and general architecture. In the next section, we challenge this discontinuity thesis and instead defend the idea of continuity between individual and institutional corruption.

3. A continuity approach

We defend the importance of stressing the common root of the institutional and the individual dimensions of political corruption against those institutionalist approaches that, drawing on the separateness explanation, emphasize the discontinuity between the two. We agree that to understand political corruption we must also consider the wider institutional framework in which this form of corruption occurs. However, we also emphasize the practical and theoretical importance of indicating the continuity between the corrupt conduct of officeholders and the corruption of the institutions in which they operate.

As seen in the previous section, the discontinuity thesis holds that—to use Lessig's plain wording—"institutions may be corrupt even if their members are not" (Lessig 2014, 2. See also Lessig 2018, 12, 19; Thompson 2018, 1). This thesis is misleading in that it fails to do justice to an institution's structural features. In particular, the idea that the distinction between individual and institutional corruption should draw only on the motivation (personal vs. political) behind corrupt actions and practices oversimplifies the description of the dynamics of political corruption. Challenging the discontinuity view, the continuity thesis that we defend explains how institutional corruption can always and only be understood by spelling out the relation between the functioning of institutional roles and the individual officeholders' uses of power. Any time we call an institution corrupt, we are actually using a shorthand expression to signify a kind of institutional *action*. Political corruption thus refers to corrupt institutional practices instantiated by the interrelated conduct of the officeholders in an institution. To be appropriately responsive to the structural features of an institution, a map of political corruption in institutional practices must follow the patterns of interrelatedness of embodied institutional roles—that is, the uses of power that officeholders make when they act in their institutional capacity. As pointed out, there is no institutional action besides those uses of power; therefore, to describe and assess institutional practices means to describe and assess the officeholders' conduct. This focus on the officeholders' interrelated institutional action allows an engagement with institutional practices and a detailed analysis of the actual patterns of the officeholders' interaction. In this way, we can go deeper into the study of the functioning of an institution than we could do by following an institutionalist approach that looks only at the formal mechanisms and general architecture of an institution and its design.[5]

In Chapter 1, we explained that specific powers of office are entrusted to the various institutional roles. Officeholders are expected to perform specific role-based functions in keeping with a mandate whose terms are generally accessible to them. The functioning of an institution reflects its raison d'être. The raison d'être of an institution comprises the normative ideals that ground its establishment and, consequently, its internal structure and functioning. Different power mandates are entrusted to different institutional roles with a view to ensuring the well-functioning of the institution as per the officeholders' interrelated work. Given these premises, a well-ordered society is one in which public institutions are well designed and well-functioning, which means their structures and procedures are conceived and work coherently with their raison d'être. We have already seen that some variations and evolutions of an institution's raison d'être are "physiological" and sometimes are due to the officeholders' role contestation.[6] However, even in conditions of stability, well-designed institutions cannot remain faithful to their raison d'être (they cannot be

---

[5] This focus differentiates our approach from that of some institutionalists such as Lessig (2018), Thompson (2018), and Weinstock (2019). It is also helpful to see the compatibility between our argument and other institutionalist theories that recognize the crucial role of institutional action in explaining political corruption, such as Miller (2017).

[6] Theorists as different as John Rawls (1971) and Jeremy Waldron (2003) subscribe to this interpretation of the role of public institutions. We revisit the issue of institutional change with reference to the contestation of powers of office in the next chapter.

well-functioning) unless officeholders exercise their powers of office in accordance with the terms of the mandate entrusted to their institutional roles. In this way, the officeholders' interrelated action can sustain the raison d'être of an institution, thus taking up the responsibility for its well-functioning across time. Instead, when officeholders fail to act in this way and their conduct is incoherent with the raison d'être of the institution, they may fail the institution in which they work and turn it, ipso facto, into something different. The institutional raison d'être is thus undermined. As anticipated in Chapter 1, political corruption is the use of an officeholder's power of office that fails a public institution in this way; therefore, officeholders may become by their conduct "internal enemies" of an institution.[7] No matter how well designed an institution may be, internal enemies may act in a way that will impede the performance of its functions and, in this sense, fail its raison d'être. [8]

To see the difference between our continuity thesis and the institutionalists' discontinuity view, consider the case of a congresswoman elected with the funds of some lobbies, among others, who on her first day of office finds a long line of those lobbyists outside her office, all of them pushing their own agenda. At the moment she listens to those lobbyists' claims, thus neglecting her own agenda or at any rate her own priorities on the basis of which citizens voted for her, political corruption occurs. However, we cannot say (the institutionalists would argue) that she is herself corrupt in the sense that she is moved by a corrupt personal motive or by a bad character trait, such as greed. As we have seen in the previous section, for such institutionalists as Lessing and Thompson,

---

[7] Negligence and incompetence are other examples of behaviors that may fail an institution's raison d'être.

[8] The tone of these considerations is intentionally descriptive and is, thus, insufficient to ground a moral assessment of the wrongness of political corruption (necessary for establishing whether failing an institution's raison d'être is always bad, even in the face of unjust or illegitimate institutions). We recognize the importance of this point (and the potentially conservative implications it may yield) and will revisit it toward the end of Chapter 3.

the congresswoman's actions are totally understandable in virtue of the mechanisms by which she got into power. Nevertheless, institutionalists are critical of the current development of the lobby system, which leads the members of Congress to be responsive to lobbies rather than to their constituency, following a principle of democratic equality.[9] In this sense, the institutional conditions in which the congresswoman operates reveal a structural *democratic* deficit. Taking our continuist approach, instead, we would say that the congresswoman does in fact act in a corrupt manner. What makes her conduct corrupt is a deficit of *office accountability* to the extent that, by prioritizing lobbyists' demands (rather than following the platform on the basis of which she got into power), the congresswoman pursues an agenda whose rationale may not be vindicated as coherent with the terms of her mandate. We can diagnose political corruption without having to express any further judgment regarding the congresswoman's personal motive or character (thus capturing the institutionalists' concerns). We can limit ourselves to attributing corruption to the congresswoman's use of her power of office at the moment she plays the lobbyists' game. Had she taken a more balanced approach to the lobbyists' demands with respect to the demands of her electoral constituency, there would be no political corruption, even if we could still say that private electoral campaign financing creates the circumstances for political corruption.

When an institution fails its raison d'être because some officeholders make use of their power of office to pursue an agenda

---

[9] Note that both Thompson's and Lessig's observations start from a political context, that of the United States, in which the work of lobbies is a lawful and normalized channel for interest representation. In this way, the effects of lobbying activities cannot be criticized as unlawful, but only because of the practices that they trigger. In particular, responsiveness to the lobbies' demands has become more important for members of Congress than responsiveness to their constituency. The institutionalists suggest that the degeneration of the lobby system is incompatible with some more fundamental values of the U.S. political system, such as democratic equality. Granted, this general characterization, the difference between the continuity and discontinuity theses, concerns the role that individual officeholders play in such a degenerative process.

whose rationale is unaccountable as incoherent with the terms of their mandate, we say that institutional action (and not only the discrete actions of those who act within the institution) is itself corrupt. In this sense, we can side with institutionalists to emphasize the importance of the institutional dimension of political corruption. But what we add, and the institutionalists fail to recognize, is that, in virtue of what an institution is (i.e., a system of *interrelated embodied* rule-governed roles), institutional failures always occur via the corrupt conduct of some of their members. For this reason, a closer look at institutional structures, the division of roles, and patterns of interrelation can reveal how institutional action may come to be itself corrupt.

Suppose, for example, that some experts working for a public agency for risk assessment are involved in authorizing the marketing of a certain product. Some of the experts deliver a favorable opinion that is officially based on scientific evidence but secretly respond to some economic incentives offered by the producer company. Some other experts express a contrary opinion based on a study that shows opposite scientific evidence, which, however, does not prevail. In this case, the agency as an institution concedes the authorization to market the product, giving credit to some false factual information about the product under examination. In our view, the agency's decision can be called corrupt because some—but certainly not all—of the agency's members used their power of office to pursue an agenda whose rationale may not be vindicated as coherent with their mandate (by responding to some economic incentives). By saying that the agency's decision is corrupt, we affirm that the agency's action has failed its raison d'être, which includes (we can assume) providing decisions based on good science.[10]

---

[10] This example refers to a case of political corruption in which the scientific evidence offered by some experts becomes the Trojan Horse of corruption in the institution. Because of the reference to use of expert knowledge, examples of this kind are sometimes interpreted as cases of "corruption of knowledge." We like to point out, however,

From this example, supporters of a discontinuity thesis would probably argue that even if it is possible to identify corrupt behavior in some cases of institutional corruption and explain its political relevance, a focus on individual misconduct does not help—generally and reliably—to produce an appropriate diagnosis of the problem at stake. It is clear, they could argue, that the relevant question to be asked is above all one about the nature of decision-making procedures, institutional mechanisms, incentive structures, and networks that favor political corruption. Given the relevance of public institutions in stabilizing the public order, it is of a paramount importance to make sense of those mechanisms, so as to be able to intervene and stop occasions for political corruption. In particular, where mechanisms and structures conducive to political corruption are identified, it seems appropriate to "draw the pond," to use Lessig's words, so as to eliminate the ecosystem in which political corruption flourishes (Lessig 2005). In reply to this, and accepting this challenge, in the next section we propose that in fact a continuity approach is particularly suited to highlight the links between institutional roles, relationships, processes, and political corruption. In this way, we are able to give a more accurate picture of the structural dynamics of political corruption in institutional practices than the one offered by drawing solely on the opposition between the nature of political processes and the

that there is only a family resemblance between political corruption and corruption of knowledge; the two expressions designate two different phenomena and problems. Problematizing the corruption of knowledge means questioning how knowledge is produced in contemporary societies. Individually and as a society, we put remarkable trust in the idea of knowledge at the service of human progress. Prominently, we think that good science can assist us in improving our practical decisions. Such trust is seemingly blind, however, to the ways knowledge is produced (Radder 2010). Powerful economic actors are in a position, for example, to sponsor and disseminate research and to reward research results congenial to specific economic interests. Thus, these economic actors have the power of "corrupting" the knowledge base of our decisions. This phenomenon is pervasive in contemporary societies and probably has not yet received the attention it deserves (but see Lessig 2018, Ch. 4). Surely, in cases in which corrupt knowledge is used in public policy, there may be intersections between corrupt knowledge and political corruption. Although we recognize the importance of these intersections, we think it is crucial to keep the two problems distinct.

officeholders' personal motives, or on considerations pertaining to institutional design only. Our proposal is to look at public institutions not as mere sets of more or less well-designed rules, mechanisms, and procedures. Instead, whether a public institution is well-functioning depends crucially on the way the officeholders who embody the institution exercise their powers of office in institutional practices.

Institutionalists committed to the discontinuity thesis have neglected this important feature of institutions. This neglect is problematic for two main reasons. First, by neglecting the condition that institutional roles are necessarily embodied (that is, occupied by humans), they lose sight of individual actions and risk upholding a form of fetishism of procedures. This problem is conceptual, but there is also a second problem, which is mainly diagnostic. On the one hand, institutionalists build into the definition of individual corruption the idea that corruption is always motivated by a personal motive (such as personal gain) or the officeholder's bad character trait (such as greed). In this way, a judgment of corrupt behavior is the same as casting a moral judgment on the character of the officeholder. On the other hand, by focusing prevalently on institutional rules, procedures, and mechanisms, institutionalists (especially those championing a separateness explanation) fail to track individual and group dynamics among the determinants of institutional corruption. In so doing, they lose sight of the many subtle and insidious ways an institution may be corrupt in virtue of the patterns of interaction that occur between its members, even when there is nothing wrong with its design (and the general rules that govern the interaction). In other words, they fail to consider that no institution can be designed in such a way that makes it immune from political corruption, which may always sneak in per the officeholders' work.

The next section shows the importance of this second problem by articulating a taxonomy of political corruption in institutional practices. This taxonomy seeks to give a systematic account of different patterns of institutional interrelatedness and is thus crucial to understanding the sense in which we mean that political corruption is an internal enemy of public institutions.

4. A taxonomy of political corruption in institutional practices

Political corruption is a particular way a public institution fails its raison d'être. Our thesis is that the phenomenology of what is generally called "institutional corruption" can be traced back to the corrupt conduct of officeholders who, through interrelatedness, fail to sustain the functioning of their institution.

We have seen that an officeholder acts corruptly when her conduct instantiates a deficit of office accountability. A deficit of office accountability occurs when an officeholder acts in her institutional capacity (the power-of-office condition of political corruption) but exercises her power of office to pursue an agenda whose rationale may not be vindicated as coherent with the terms of that power mandate (the mandate condition of political corruption). Because of the structural interrelatedness of institutional roles, the way any single officeholder uses her power of office is relevant for the performance of others' roles and, therefore, for the capacity of an institution to be faithful to its raison d'être (i.e., to be well-functioning). In this sense, the corrupt officeholders' conduct is an "internal enemy" that transforms even well-designed institutions into corrupt ones. So to say that political corruption is in institutional practices does not merely indicate the condition in which the rules that govern an institution are systematically violated. It is not even just a shorthand expression to designate either the structural (rather than personal) causes of political corruption (as the substrate explanation suggests) or its institutional consequences—such that individual corrupt behavior becomes politically relevant only to the extent that it causes an institution to stray from its purpose, as the teleological explanation has it. Instead, we identify corrupt institutional action with a deficit of office accountability that occurs, via interrelatedness, in virtue of the conduct of those officeholders who by their action fail the raison d'être of their institution.

Because of the interrelatedness of institutional roles, there is no case of individual corruption on the part of an officeholder that is not also institutional. This twofold nature of political corruption does not hold merely in virtue of a causal relation between the individual and the institutional dimensions of this phenomenon. Unlike the proponents of the teleological and the substrate explanations, the link we see between these two dimensions is "constitutive." This means that any time an officeholder acts in a corrupt manner (as we described it), his very conduct *is* (and does not merely entail) a failure of the institution's raison d'être. This is because the power mandates assigned to each and every institutional role are established in keeping with the institution's raison d'être, and their realization is in this sense constitutes an institution's well-functioning. We can thus see how political corruption constitutes certain "damaged" institutional practices rather than being merely causally related to them.

Because the relationships between officeholders that link individual corrupt conduct to corrupt institutional practices are qualitatively and quantitatively diverse, we next present three different patterns of continuity, which correspond to three models of political corruption in institutional practices. To map the variety of patterns that this form of corruption may consist of, we distinguish between a *summative*, a *morphological*, and a *systemic* model of political corruption in institutional practices (Ferretti 2019).

4.1 Summative corruption

The first kind of political corruption in institutional practices has a summative character. When many of the individuals embodying an institution act in a corrupt way, we may say that institutional action is itself corrupt.

How many corrupt officeholders are necessary in order to have institutional corruption is an empirical question. What matters is that in this case the sum of corrupt individual behaviors "hits" the institution in its very raison d'être. For example, if a border official allows, upon payment of a bribe, the smuggling of bulk cash, proceeds of drug trafficking may cross the border. If a good number of inspectors regularly allow bulk-cash smuggling, this will become a safe channel for money smugglers, and an informal bribe-and-smuggle practice will characterize the work of the agency, which will then cease to be well-functioning. The conduct of the border officials, taken as members of the same institution, makes the border-control agency unable to impede money smuggling—as, in fact, coherence with its raison d'être would demand. The political salience of this form of corruption does not only concern the cumulative consequences of a number of severe individual corrupt actions occurring over time. In cases of summative corruption, what matters is not just the condition that many individual officeholders happen to be corrupt, but that their actions, taken together, fail the raison d'être of the agency in such a way that makes it no longer a border-control agency by curtailing its well-functioning. Once the informal bribe-and-smuggle practice is established, the agency's institutional action, and not just the discrete actions of the officeholders taken in isolation, is corrupt.

The diagnosis of institutional corruption demands that we look at causal relations between individual conduct and institutional functioning, and also at patterns of interaction of different officeholders to see how they sum up and fail the raison d'être of the institution. In this sense, we think that institutionalists may find the taxonomy useful for the diagnosis of some causal dynamic that links individual and institutional corrupt practices. However, as we will show, a closer look at different instances of interrelatedness reveals cases in which the property of corruption applies to the institution as a whole and is irreducible to the conduct of its members, severally taken, and the causality between their actions.

4.2 Morphological corruption

There are cases of political corruption in institutional practices that cannot be explained by the aggregation of discrete acts of individual misconduct. These cases, as we show in this section, can be understood only by focusing on the interrelatedness of the differentiated institutional roles and the constellations in which officeholders exercise their power mandate in a particular institution.

To see these cases, recall that, by the interrelatedness of institutional roles, the tasks and obligations attached to each role cannot be discharged if not in coordination (or in relationships of subordination in a hierarchy) with others. This is a structural feature of institutional action, in the context of which each officeholder is both empowered and constrained in her conduct. Because of this interrelatedness, corruption of one particular officeholder may also imply that other officeholders are incapacitated to perform the tasks entrusted to their roles.

Consider, for example, the case of an administrator who is tasked to select a pool of experts for advice on the weighted dangers of a new pharmaceutical product. The drug producer bribes the administrator to appoint an expert who can deliver a favorable scientific opinion. Because it involves a bribe, this is a classic case of an officeholder's individual corruption. Suppose now that other officeholders are called to decide on the marketing authorization for that pharmaceutical product. They base their judgment on the expert's report and find evidence in support of the marketing authorization. In doing so, they act according to the rules of their office (what we called the letter of their mandate). The spirit of the entire procedure, however, has been compromised by the corrupt conduct of one bribed administrator, and the institution as a whole thus fails its raison d'être. When used in this sense, political corruption can be attributed to the action of a group of people constituting a public institution in the same way synchrony can be attributed to, say, rhythmic gymnasts when they morph into a cohesive group. It may take just one individual to distort the shape that the group will take. Because of the conduct of one member, the athletes as a group may in fact be doing something different from what they had been planning to do. In the eyes of an external observer, the athletes succeed or fail as a group in their interrelatedness, even if the failure is due to the conduct of one single gymnast. This is what we call *morphological corruption*. In this case, even if not all, or not even the majority, of the members of an institution act in a corrupt manner, their activity as a group is corrupt. Because of their corrupt colleague, the performance of other officeholders is also different from what it should be. So, in the same way that the gymnasts may be performing a different exercise because of one single athlete who is not synchronized with the rest, officeholders in an institution working together may fail the raison d'être of their institution in virtue of the corrupt conduct of one of their colleagues.

Another possibility is that one of our gymnasts makes a mistake and others, in response, readjust their own performance with marginal changes. Although the end result may look slightly better to the observer than complete asynchrony, it still is noticeably different from the original plan. Analogously, cases of political corruption in institutional practices may be indicative of the readjustment of the institution faced with an act of individual corruption. For example, the dean of an academic school harbors the suspicion that a recruitment procedure in one of the school's departments was tainted by favoritism because of a possible conflict of interest. As it happens, one member of the selection committee was involved in the mentorship of the selected candidate, while this candidate was a PhD student in another university. However, the dean decides not to act on this suspicion in order not to attribute too much importance to an isolated (and possibly harmless) episode, which—should it be publicized—might cast a negative light on the fairness and impartiality of the school's hiring practices as a whole. The other colleagues in the department decide not to speak up, too, so as to avoid unpleasant controversies. Rumors about the possible instance of favoritism, however, start circulating, which creates the impression across other departments that the threshold of alertness on conflict of interests has been lowered. By gradual readjustments, this kind of practice also comes to be considered acceptable across the school for other types of conflicts of interest that could lead to favoritism. While the details of the relation between individual and institutional corruption may vary, what matters for the "morphological diagnosis" of political corruption is the structure of the officeholders' interactions and how they change the nature of an institutional practice.

4.3 Systemic corruption

The corrupt conduct of some officeholders may give rise to a parallel institutional practice that replaces the one established in keeping with the institution's raison d'être. This form of institutional corruption corresponds to so-called systemic corruption and describes configurations of informal practices and networks that make corrupt equilibria resilient to political reform and judicial prosecution (see Della Porta and Vannucci 2012. In the present section, we focus on the structure of systemic corruption to show its common roots with individual corruption and the two models of political corruption in institutional practices described earlier.

From the structural point of view, cases of systemic corruption are often a combination of summative and morphological instances of political corruption that ramify across several interconnected institutions and become a veritable social activity, rather than being limited to some episodic acts of isolated individuals or small groups. As for all other cases of political corruption in institutional practices, at the core of systemic corruption is the corrupt conduct of an individual and its interplay with the conduct of other officeholders, interconnected via institutional relations. The difference between systemic corruption and the previously discussed models is that the relations, mutual incentives, and interconnections leading to political corruption are so intricate that, looking retrospectively, it is generally impossible to point to any specific corrupt action of an officeholder as the source of political corruption. We see the wood and we know there are trees, but it is difficult to distinguish them for what they are.

A typical case is a corrupt system of public procurement. Political corruption can manifest itself in public procurement in many ways. However, for simplicity, consider the issue of tenders. Many governmental agencies require that calls for tenders be widely advertised so as to encourage competition and provide a greater pool of offers to select from and to give all potential tenderers a fair chance of making a successful offer. The offer that best meets all requirements and provides value for money should win the contract. However, as a matter of practice, in many cases, respondents know that the purchasing officials involved are corruptible. For example, it may be known that a tenderer, after payment of a bribe, can submit a low bid with the understanding that the officials in charge of the contract implementation and audit will approve later price increases or amendments to the original contract.[11]

In this context, the actions of the officeholders who are in charge of the bid evaluation need not necessarily be themselves corrupt: Contract renegotiation at a later stage may not even involve the administrative employees who were in the original corrupt relation. The substantial renegotiation of the contract may be introduced in the form of a number of incremental changes that may be approved, for example, by on-site engineers. In each particular

---

[11] For an illustration of such irregularities and corrupt practices in tender procedures, see, for example, Chiodelli (2019).

case, the corrupt practice of the low bid may be introduced at some point by some agents under payment of a bribe. However, where political corruption has a systemic character, the individual conduct of some is the initial item in a long transformative process in which a multiplicity of corrupt reward mechanisms can no longer be traced back to the actions of the corrupt officeholders who initiated it. It may be, for example, that direct bribing no longer plays a role, but a system of reticence and fear of scandals provides incentives for officeholders not to expose the new practice that is de facto followed in their institution or even a system of connected institutions. In response to that transformation, bidders may have formed a cartel to minimize the costs of participating in a tender and to pressure purchasing officials to apply the rule of the low bid while either having internal agreements in place to compensate for failed bids or assigning turns for winning public tenders. For officeholders, this may facilitate the contract-selection phase because there is just one clearly winning proposal. In this scenario, all the involved officehoders—across institutions—follow a practice that is substantially and fundamentally different from the one originally established to ensure fairness in public tenders. The practice of selecting the best offer in terms of value for money is subverted and enduringly invalidated, and the ruling practice is that of the low bid. Tenderers who make cost-realistic offers will be regularly outbid. The officeholders thus have incentives to adapt to a corrupt institutional practice. Importantly, they do it without following ipso facto what most institutionalists would consider a corrupt motive or thereby necessarily reveal a corrupt trait of their character. This specification is important because one of the main preoccupations of institutionalists such as Lessig (2018) is to rescue participants in corrupt institutional practices from themselves being called corrupt.

With regard to our model of systemic corruption, to say that a system is corrupt at the structural level is to identify a double institutional practice: the formal practice that officially governs an institution (in keeping with its raison d'être) and the informal practice that the corrupt system has established. Where political corruption becomes the governing practice, it prospers in a way that is parasitical on the official one. The corrupt officeholders have incentives to maintain the official practice formally in place. This is the basis of their unofficial power (which exceeds the power entrusted to their role via an institutional mandate) because it allows corrupt practices to prosper over time. We see this pattern in action across several institutional areas and in various institutional practices such as nepotism in academic hierarchies or clientelism in the provision of public services.

To be sure, such cases could be the object of contestation, say, by citizens who may denounce an institution that awards too expensive contracts. This reaction is much harder, however, when these contracts are the outcome of a (formally fair) tendering procedure. Of interest here is that political corruption, on the one hand, awards privileges to some (in terms of public contracts) and, on the other hand, escapes standard answerability. So, it is possible to identify who benefits from political corruption individually, but it is very difficult to indicate who should be singled out to respond for establishing and maintaining the corrupt practice. While in "pure" summative or morphological cases it is possible to identify the agents of political corruption, systemic cases present a complexity such that it is difficult to isolate and assess specific contributions and establish whose responsibilities are sufficient to warrant culpability. Many theorists have insisted on systemic aspects as opposed to individualist approaches in part to overcome the difficulty of assigning individual responsibilities in cases of systemic corruption. However, as we argue more extensively in Chapter 4, the difficulty cannot simply disappear by readjusting the lens and taking a wider perspective. It is, rather, by investigating from a closer distance the complexity of the links, relations, and interconnectedness between the actions of the officeholders that responsibility for political corruption can also be assigned in systemic cases.

5. A case of systemic corruption

Consider political corruption in a large-scale public construction project. This kind of case is often said to be paradigmatic of systemic corruption because the patterns of corruption are typically so entrenched in the system that they look impossible to avoid despite the efforts of many well-intended individual actors.[12] We now show how our approach based on a continuity thesis enables a precise diagnosis of political corruption.

The case is that of the construction of the Berlin Brandenburg Willy Brandt Airport in Germany. Since the very beginning of this construction project in 2006, it has been plagued by cost overruns and delays. It was originally budgeted to cost 2.5 billion Euros and to open in 2012, but it was inaugurated only in October 2020, eight years behind schedule, at a cost of up to three times the original estimate.

The airport project was commissioned by the Flughafen Berlin Brandenburg GmbH (FBB), which is owned by the federal states of Berlin and Brandenburg (37% each) and the Federal Republic of Germany (the remaining 26%). On the project supervisory board sit mainly politicians representative of the various ruling political parties at both state and federal levels.

The airport was planned to become the third-largest airport in Germany, and hundreds of companies were to take on subcontracts in the complex construction works. In this context, the Dutch Engineering and Consultancy agency Royal Imtech, which is involved in the construction of a number of public buildings in Germany, played a key role as an interlocutor for the project supervisory board and as a kind of umbrella organization under which a number of other companies operated. Imtech became

---

[12] A number of reports from nongovernmental organizations (NGOs) and professional associations target large-scale public projects as one of the most conspicuous sources of political corruption. See, for example, Robertson, Atherton, and Moses (2015).

the motor of a system of corruption, first revealed by an investigation in spring 2015. The investigators identified the way Imtech influenced the project development as a "planned chaos," in which original specifications were changed in the course of the work so as to create supplementary costs. These changes caused delays, technical mistakes, and costly reworking.

The way public prosecutors have reconstructed the dynamics of corruption follows the typical legal approach of trying to single out individual responsibilities. A department head at the airport, on payment of a bribe of €150,000, first arranged the unmonitored payment of Imtech invoices totaling €65 million. In December 2012, the airport's in-house auditors questioned one large invoice filed by Imtech, and the legal department found that only €18 million of the €33 million invoice was justified. However, speaking before the airport supervisory board, the airport's chief operating officer, Horst Amann, pointed out that the sum was necessary to meet the construction deadline, which led the board to approve a transfer of €22 million. Only during the investigation would the audit office admit to have failed to hold the airport management to its responsibility. Similarly, other actors involved at different stages of the implementation of the project admitted their mistakes. However, the project had required such a great investment of capital (especially from public funds, including from the European Union) and of political effort (to increase the social acceptability of the construction especially for the people living close to the airport) that the prospect of having to abandon it was the worst and most embarrassing scenario for everyone involved.

Most of the politicians and public officials supporting the project had linked their personal reputations to the timely and successful completion of the airport and, therefore, had little interest in drawing attention to any potential scandals or in stopping the construction work in order to allow stricter financial review. In turn, Imtech justified inflated costs on the grounds of supplementary and accelerated construction costs. At the same time, the contract was vital for Imtech as the company was experiencing heavy financial difficulties, which were also a threat to subcontractors. Probably for these reasons, suspicions of irregularity were silenced. Despite the attempts to fill financial gaps, Imtech went bankrupt on August 13, 2015. Meanwhile, besides the trial for corruption of the responsible officials, a number of people responsible for the airport project resigned and others have taken over their role. They did not, however, find a convincing solution to the problem of completing construction, which was postponed for years.

Some reflections are in order here. The airport officer's bribe is of course at the core of the legal investigation, although the judges stated that it could not be established whether the initiative came from Imtech's representatives or was solicited by the airport officer.[13] However, establishing this point is relatively uninteresting in the context of the subsequent events because clearly the category of individual corruption cannot tell the whole story in a way that accounts for the complexity of the dynamics of political corruption in place. Imtech perfected a system that proved very difficult to neutralize, even after the prosecution of those individuals, who, driven by a corrupt motive, are known to have committed irregularities, both technically and legally, and after the resignation of others who admitted their failure to control the project adequately.

The accounting fraud, failures to comply with safety requirements, and inflated costs for customers (including Audi, RWE, and Siemens) are just part of the problem. This scandal unveiled a range of enduring shady practices and exchanges involving a number of other public construction projects in which some contractors and subcontractors were deemed to have inflated construction costs by threatening customers with technical problems and delays in construction. These included Germany's largest railway project, Stuttgart 21, in which Imtech participated in 2013–15. The corrupt routines were so entrenched in the

---

[13] Landgericht Cottbus Az. 22 KLs 8/15 and ZAP EN-Nr. 73/2017.

system that they seem to have survived even Imtech's bankruptcy. This complexity suggests that big construction projects are often accompanied by corruption scandals and that an appropriate diagnosis must go beyond the logic of individual rule violation, which can only capture a tiny part of the problem at stake.

Some institutionalists may say that large construction works are a fertile substrate for political corruption. This interpretation can help us to see that very often we can spot political corruption in the occurrence of construction works, especially when they are parts of a large project that involves many actors whose work is difficult to coordinate and supervise. The supervision of contractors requires technical skills that very often are missing in public officers sitting on boards, and financial control is often passed on to specialized bodies, which can only rely on reports on the progress of works prepared by some technical committees. In this sense, the substrate explanation can be usefully employed to identify those institutional practices that are particularly susceptible to corruption. However, the identification of some general difficulties surrounding the management of large construction works cannot, on its own, make sense of concrete cases of political corruption such as the one under examination. Instead, we suggest viewing the substrate explanation as the first step of an analysis of actual violations, threats, and offers—all being patterns of interrelatedness between the various actors involved that make the airport construction an actual case of political corruption in an institutional practice. The three models of political corruption in institutional practices illustrated earlier provide the full diagnostic toolkit for such an analysis.

The teleological explanation could have the advantage of focusing on the damages of political corruption to institutional functioning. By pointing to the inflated construction costs and delays in construction works, it is possible to say that the airport project as such has deviated from its purposes. However, when we try to identify the causal dynamics leading to those effects, we are inevitably faced with competing purposes. So, from a teleological perspective, a first difficulty is to establish which unit of institutional corruption and which purposes are relevant for the diagnosis of political corruption. For example, while the financial office was interested in complying with the original budget, for the management board the additional costs were the price to pay for the ultimate goal of completing the project as promised. The enormous delays in construction works and the failure to meet safety standards were part of a system of inflating costs that held both the members of the supervisory board and the officials of the technical affairs office hostages of their public commitment to ensure the success of the airport project.

Let us turn now to the reason why the supporters of a separateness explanation would consider it inadequate to focus the diagnosis of the Willy Brandt Airport case on the individual conduct of those who triggered the corruption of the airport project. We have already pointed out the difficulty of establishing the causal links between an individual corrupt conduct and the institutional damages it may cause in the light of some institutional purposes. But even if identifying single corrupt actions were possible, we might risk overlooking the very dynamics that were benefiting the institution (ensuring that progress in the construction works was made) and at the same time making it deviate from its purposes and original commitments (by paying disproportionate costs). From this perspective, the most serious aspect is that Imtech was able to keep public officials hostages in a corrupt web of relationships by drawing on the contractors' need to see the construction works completed. To see this aspect, it seems plausible to conceive of individual and institutional corruption as two separate ideas and phenomena. We concur that adopting this perspective helps make sense of the fact that most of the actors involved were not moved by personal corrupt motives but instead served institutional goals. However, were we to refer only to institutional purposes and mechanisms without pointing out the specific economic and political relations among the numerous actors involved and the technical complexity of this particular project, we would be unable to explain how political corruption could take place at all. This is why the separateness explanation of systemic corruption cannot offer a sufficiently accurate diagnosis of the complexities of the case.

In sum, we have shown that, viewed individually, the substrate, the teleological, and the separateness explanations of institutional corruption, though useful in bringing into focus some important aspects of the case we have scrutinized, cannot capture the full complexity of corrupt relational patterns that make the airport project such an exemplary case of systemic corruption. The core of the matter is not only that specific objectives have been missed, or that large construction projects are generally at high risk of corruption, but that an individual action has inaugurated a corrupt organizational practice, which has substantially changed the airport project, thus failing its raison d'être. Our proposal is that the most appropriate illustration of the structure of this case pinpoints the continuity between the conduct of the different officeholders, taken in the context of the interrelatedness of their roles within a complex institutional structure, and the establishment of some institutional practice over time. Thus, we can understand the gravity of the initial bribe only by contextualizing it within a broader institutional setting and pointing at the web of relations between the various actors in view of the involvement of the politicians on the board and their promises to citizens concerning completing the airport construction works.

The technical complexity and the relative difficulties in exercising supervision of the ensuing web of contractors and subcontractors explain the problems the financial auditors encountered when trying to differentiate between reasonable and unreasonable additional costs. To appreciate this complexity, we must focus on the interrelatedness of the different institutional roles and the uses of their mandate as well as the relative power implicated throughout the process. This focus goes beyond the piecemeal observation of the cumulative effects of several individual actions. Moreover, it requires a more substantial analysis than one based on the design of formal mechanisms and procedures. Notably, our continuity-based approach sheds light on the constellations of institutional relations between the unaccountable conducts of various officeholders within the context of institutional procedures and mechanisms, thus going beyond the separate assessment of either individual corrupt behaviors or institutional mechanisms and procedures. An assessment of institutional practices, as we have shown, should include not only causal dynamics and individual actions, but also morphological configurations in virtue of which officeholders, who do not themselves act for a corrupt motive, may contribute to failing an institution's raison d'être. To disentangle these diverse relations and dynamics is not only useful to reach a better understanding of cases of systemic corruption, but also, as we argue in the following chapters, to assess responsibilities for and elaborate adequate responses to political corruption.

6. Conclusion

In everyday language, we often attribute corruption to an institution, and institutionalists have made the case for focusing on institutions as a unit of study in a diagnosis of political corruption. As we have seen in this chapter, part of the motivation for this case draws on the consideration that when an individual's corrupt conduct has an effect on an institutional practice, that conduct acquires a special importance because it hinders the pursuit of institutional goals (teleological explanation). But institutionalists have also pointed out that the individual involvement in corrupt institutional practices may be a further source of corruption. From this point of view, corrupt institutional practices offer the incentives for and the substrate in which corrupt behaviors may prosper (substrate explanation).

We agree that the quality and quantity of the institutional consequences of individual corrupt behavior are relevant in a number of political, social, and economic analyses and that a focus on the institutional causes or the circumstances that favor individual corruption may help to identify environments more exposed to the risk of becoming corrupt. However, we have also argued that, to appreciate the complexity of these links between the individual and the institutional dimensions of political corruption, we must focus on the structural-relational aspects of this phenomenon in virtue of the interrelatedness of institutional roles and of the relative exercises of powers of office. To see these aspects, we must reject the discontinuity thesis, according to which individual and institutional corruption are discontinuous concepts and phenomena (the separateness explanation of institutional corruption), so that we may find institutional corruption even in the absence of a corrupt individual action.

We have instead grounded our analysis of political corruption on a continuity thesis that emphasizes the common conceptual and practical root of the individual and the institutional dimensions of this phenomenon. Drawing on the idea of the interrelatedness between the roles constituting an institution, we have proposed three models that explain different ways in which political corruption can be attributed to an institutional practice in virtue of the structural relations between those who exercise their powers of office within it. Analysis of the institutional conduct of officeholders is not only able to explain political corruption as a property of an institutional practice but also to specify its diagnosis with reference to concrete individual actions.

Our continuity-based approach to political corruption has shown how political corruption is rooted in the corrupt conduct of individual officeholders, interconnected through their institutional roles. Insofar as (some of) those who act in those roles make use of their power of office to pursue an agenda whose rationale may not be vindicated as coherent with the terms of their power mandate (deficit of office accountability), they fail the raison d'être of the institution within which they operate and, therefore, institutional action is itself corrupt.

There is no corrupt institutional practice that falls outside the summative, morphological, and systemic models that we have identified in §4. It may be possible to devise submodels for a more accurate differentiation of different empirical cases, or to find overlapping areas between the different models (especially in cases of systemic corruption). However, we think that our taxonomy provides the complete basic toolkit for the structural analysis of political corruption in institutional practices.

Our discussion so far has been entirely descriptive. The normative implications of this continuity thesis for assessing the wrongness of political corruption and the relevance of our taxonomy for assigning responsibility for political corruption are presented in Chapters 3 and 4, respectively.

3

How is political corruption wrong?

1. Introduction

In the first part of this book, we offered a philosophical analysis of political corruption as a deficit of office accountability and presented the twofold (individual and institutional) dimension in which this form of corruption occurs. In carrying out this analysis, we have kept a neat descriptive focus. The time has now come to explain how and why corrupt uses of powers of office are *wrong* and what normative implications ensue for assigning moral *responsibilities* for corruption and anticorruption. The first task motivates the present chapter; we attend to the second task in the subsequent chapters.

Throughout the normative discussion of political corruption, we defend a *deontological* approach to its wrongness. This approach must be seen as an integration (not an alternative) to the many forms of consequentialism that represent the mainstream as concerns the assessment of political corruption. The consequentialist approach has standardly emphasized the dependence of any normative judgment of political corruption on its (expected or actual) measurable negative consequences for a polity's economic, political, and social life, or because it undermines an institution's integrity by distracting it from its defining purpose. In this chapter, we contend that this approach, in all its variants, is insufficient on its own to make sense of the common claim that political corruption is a wrongful use of power. This claim is central to any discussion of the wrongness of political corruption in the scholarly as well

Political Corruption. Emanuela Ceva and Maria Paola Ferretti, Oxford University Press (2021). © Oxford University Press. DOI: 10.1093/oso/9780197567869.003.0004

as public debate, and yet its analysis is almost taken for granted by a focus on consequences or institutional purposes.

In this chapter, we show how and why political corruption is normatively relevant as a problem of public ethics even when such negative implications are absent or unclear. In Chapter 1, we illustrated how political corruption cannot be exclusively *defined* by its consequences; in this chapter, we argue that, similarly, it should not be so *assessed*. By presenting an integrative deontological normative assessment of political corruption, we introduce in the debate a fundamental sense in which this form of unaccountable use of a power of office is inherently wrong—without thereby denying that when it *also* has negative consequences, it may become even more practically urgent to address.

To say that political corruption is itself a problem of public ethics shows that its assessment relies on the normative principles that ought to guide the individual conduct and institutional practices through which powers of office are exercised. In this sense, the guidance is *public,* concerning the *actions* of officeholders—taken both severally and in their interrelatedness—rather than *personal,* concerning the *character* traits of the individuals who happen to hold institutional roles. Thus, our argument shows no traces of perfectionism or moralism. By following this path, we highlight the primary duty of a public ethics of office that political corruption inherently violates, thus paving the way to think about the institutional responses to such violations.

In this chapter, after presenting the consequentialist assessment of political corruption across a variety of fields (§2), we offer a relational characterization of the inherent wrongness of political corruption from a deontological point of view, by insisting on the interrelatedness of institutional roles. In this light, we present the inherent wrongness of political corruption as a form of "interactive injustice" (Ceva 2016). We argue that political corruption is inherently unjust because it constitutes a violation of the duty of office accountability (§3). This duty normatively qualifies the terms of the officeholders' interaction within a public institutional setting. Political corruption is a failure to act on this duty, and, therefore, it is interactively unjust, regardless of any negative, actual, or foreseeable consequences. We proceed by qualifying the scope of our deontological normative assessment of political corruption, and we show its advantages by contrasting it with recent impartiality-based and democratic-equality-based approaches (§4). We conclude by showing the positive side of our argument as illustrating a public ethics of office accountability for public institutions (§5).

2. Consequentialist assessments of political corruption

Imagine Louise, a newly elected politician, who appoints her husband, Matthew, as her chief of staff. Imagine further that Louise appoints him irrespective of his competence or past experience, but only because of their spousal relation, which Louise thinks is being threatened by an affair she believes Matthew is having with a colleague at his current workplace. By making Matthew her chief of staff, Louise hopes to move her husband away from his supposed lover and win him back. This case of familism is an instance of political corruption. Because the agenda that informs Louise's conduct in her institutional capacity responds to a familial logic, its rationale is incoherent with the terms of the mandate with which the power of appointment was presumably entrusted to her institutional role. But how is Louise's corrupt use of her power of office wrong?

A first way to assess the wrongness of Louise's corrupt use of her power of office starts by looking at the formal rules of office that regulate her power mandate and the legal provisions that qualify it. In this sense, this instance of political corruption is wrong to the extent that it entails an unlawful action.[1] From this legal point of view,

---

[1] For a standard formulation of this approach, see La Palombara (1994).

the wrongness of corruption may also extend beyond the violation of a specific rule; It comprises the negative impact of lawbreaking on the stability of the rule of law and the general governance of a polity, especially in cases of systemic corruption.

An economic assessment of the wrongness of our case of familism, for its part, would point at the costs that Louise's corrupt use of her power of office entails for the provision of some public services, for example, in terms of inefficiency. Considering that Louise is not gaining any private economic benefit from the appointment of her husband, her conduct is wrong only insofar as Matthew turns out not to be capable of fulfilling his role, thus causing measurable economic damage to the community. More generally, from this economic point of view, the particular kind of use of power in which political corruption consists is a source of preoccupation when it impedes the efficient performance of institutional roles and, therefore, either entails a waste of public money or has impoverishing implications for the population (or a part of it). So, for example, political corruption is wrong when it is an obstacle to providing public services and economic growth as well as a deterrent to foreign investments, especially in developing countries (Jain 2001). It is in this sense that the president of the World Bank, Jim Yong Kim, has famously recognized corruption as "public enemy no. 1" (Reuters 2013). It is also in this sense that Transparency International has considered the magnitude of political corruption in a number of its reports.[2]

Consequentialist accounts of the wrongness of political corruption have also been offered by political philosophers and political scientists. They have primarily focused on the negative impact of political corruption on the quality of institutions.[3] In

---

[2] Transparency International's 2004 *Global Corruption Report* on political corruption, for instance, focuses on illicit monetary flows and their negative impact on citizens' rights and opportunities (Transparency International 2004). For a discussion of the economic costs of corruption, see also Rose-Ackerman (1999).

[3] In line with our general approach in this book, in what follows we focus on *philosophical* discussions of the wrongness of political corruption. For an institutionalist

political philosophy, consequentialist theories look for the moral justification of institutions in the ends or the actual or expected consequences of their establishment. Derivatively, they also focus on institutional mechanisms and officeholders' actions that contribute to realizing those ends. Officeholders' duties (and rights) derive from a general moral obligation to act in such a way that leads to a certain state of affairs considered of value, whose realization qualifies the end that institutional action should pursue. So, for example, to the extent that the end of hospitals is to protect individual and public health, the quality of those institutions depends entirely on their capacity to provide good health care. And so it goes for schools as providers of education, or for a parliamentary assembly as concerns, say, the justice of its decisions.

The consequentialist approach has two variants. One variant is a straightforward form of consequentialism and is typically found in utilitarian normative theories. These theories assess the quality of institutions in view of the normative properties of the state of affairs they generate, whose value is *exogenous* to the action that has generated it. So, the value of hospitals capable of protecting individual and public health by providing good health care resides in their causal contribution, say, to maximization of the overall well-being of the community where they operate. The normative criterion for assessing the quality of an institution (e.g., its contribution to social well-being) is exogenous in the sense that it is external to institutional action and generally valuable in its own right. Institutions are more or less fungible instruments for achieving this independently valuable state of affairs. In this view, political corruption is wrong to the extent that it stands in the way of a public institution's ability to perform this instrumental role (in keeping with the economic reasoning expounded earlier). Therefore, it produces (or can be expected to produce) negative externalities.

approach within the field of political science, see, for example, Della Porta and Vannucci (2012).

The second variant of consequentialism treats the value of the state of affairs generated by an institution as *endogenous* to the action that has generated it.[4] This approach qualifies teleological normative theories of political corruption, which discuss institutional failures by assessing whether and to what degree an institution can achieve its defining purpose (or telos). From this perspective, the value of hospitals capable of protecting individual and public health by providing good health care resides in the good of health care itself whose realization motivates establishing the institution and determining its mechanisms. The normative criterion for assessing the quality of an institution is endogenous in that it is internal to institutional action and gives meaning to it by qualifying its defining purpose. In this view, political corruption is wrong to the extent that it impairs institutional action by deviating from its defining purpose; therefore, it deprives a public institution of its meaning and, ultimately, undermines its integrity.

This teleological assessment is the elected approach of the institutionalist interpretations of political corruption we reviewed in Chapter 2. Some of these institutionalist accounts have adopted what we have called a *continuity thesis* by insisting on the institutional effects of the joint actions of single officeholders. Others have embraced a *discontinuity position* and have centered their normative assessments of political corruption on the decay and loss of integrity of public institutions in virtue of their internal mechanisms, even in the absence of individual corrupt personal motives. We have already sketched the structural differences between these models as they describe the dynamics of political corruption in institutional practices. As noted earlier, we have done so with reference to the work of Seumas Miller (2017), as an illustration of the first variant of the institutionalist approach, and to the work of Lawrence Lessig (2004, 2013, 2015, 2018) and Dennis Thompson (1995, 2005, 2018), who have set the canon for the second variant.

---

[4] For a discussion of these variants, see, for example Vallentyne (1988).

We will now revisit them by focusing on the normative aspects of their approaches.

Miller (2017, 16, 23, 106) builds on a teleological account of institutions as organizations constituted by the multilayered joint action of human beings, who act cooperatively in their capacity as officeholders (i.e., the occupants of institutional roles) to provide collective goods that are definitive of the institution itself. So, the police is defined by its being oriented to produce the collective good of security; hospitals are geared toward securing health care; universities, toward education; and so on. Institutional corruption occurs when a pattern of officeholders' joint actions causes the institution to deviate from its purpose (Miller 2017, 17, 68 ff., 82). To the extent that this deviation undermines the provision of a collective good, institutional corruption is wrong.

As representative instances of institutional corruption, Miller (2017, 106–18) mentions such practices as bribery, fraud, and nepotism. His discussion of nepotism is of particular relevance in assessing the case of familism with which we started this section. Nepotism is wrong—from Miller's teleological perspective—insofar as, by favoring someone on the basis of kinship, an officeholder uses her position as a means to realize her special obligations toward her personal network to the detriment of those instrumental in producing some collective good (Miller 2017, 110–15).[5] Because the case of familism whereby Louise hires her husband, Matthew, as her chief of staff only to salvage their spousal relation is a subspecies of nepotism, we can see why this case can be wrong from this institutionalist perspective. It is wrong when and to the extent that Louise's corrupt decision undermines some relevant institutional purpose concerning production of a collective good (e.g., because Matthew is incompetent).[6]

[5] For a discussion of the conflict between personal duties and duties of office as threatening an officeholder's integrity, see Mendus (2009, 43–44).
[6] Sandel (2013) offers an interpretation of political corruption along these lines. For a recent historical account of the teleological approach to political corruption from a republican perspective, see Sparling (2019).

Other institutionalists have approached the question of the wrongness of political corruption by examining those occasions when an institution loses its *integrity* independently of the corrupt personal motives of those who operate within it.[7] In this context, "integrity" means "being true to one's own character," which, from a teleological perspective, indicates an institution that fulfills its purpose.[8] Building on Thompson's work (1995, 2005), Lessig (2004, 2013, 2015, 2018) has recently consolidated an institutionalist position according to which a public institution is corrupt when it deviates from its essential purpose to the *political* (not only personal) advantage of some individual or group.

Reconsider the standard interpretation Thompson and Lessig give to the private financing of electoral campaigns. Recall from Chapter 2 that, for Lessig, the structural dependence of a politician on a wealthy donor who finances the politician's electoral campaign is corrupt because, while it appears to serve the purpose of the institution of democratic elections (by securing democratic support), in fact it ends up undercutting it. In cases of institutional corruption, the agents that engage in corrupt institutional practices need not show a corrupt character or a corrupt motive. So, a politician who receives a large donation for his campaign from a private pharmaceutical company does not obtain any material benefit for himself personally. This politician can be a "good soul" who by his conduct contributes to the corruption of an entire system. In this reading, the institution of democratic elections loses its integrity because it relies on a mechanism that creates incentives for institutional action influenced by powers other than those on whom it was designed to depend (i.e., financial groups vs. the people), thus deviating from its purpose. This form of dependence is definitive of institutional corruption, which is wrong to the extent

---

[7] Thompson (2018, 2) accounts for this essential feature by describing institutional corruption as "impersonal."

[8] This is the "identity" view of integrity presented in Calhoun (1995).

that it instantiates a democratic deficit with the *consequence* of diminishing institutional trustworthiness (Lessig 2013, 553; 2018, 25–26, 32–33; Thompson 2018, 10–11).

We have thus seen how the family of consequentialist approaches to political corruption includes assessments based on the negative economic, legal, and sociopolitical consequences of this phenomenon, as well as its negative impact on either individual or institutional morality (for an overview, see Uslaner 2015). This internal variety notwithstanding, all theories within this family converge on assessing the wrongness of political corruption by reference to its negative causal implications, be they exogenous or endogenous to institutional action.[9] This consequentialist approach can make sense of a significant *part* of our moral intuitions concerning the wrongness of political corruption.

However, we also believe that there is an important dimension of the wrongness of political corruption that may not be reduced to its negative consequences, either within or outside the institution itself. To understand this dimension, we must recognize that in many instances of political corruption the consequences of individual corrupt behavior or institutional practices may be either absent or, most likely, unclear, difficult to measure or weigh against other costs and possible benefits, or unforeseeable across the many instances and contexts in which this form of corruption may occur. Corrupt uses of the power of office may or may not entail lawbreaking, and the assessment of their economic costs and political impact is volatile. Institutional purposes themselves are hardly straightforward or unequivocally identified; rather, they are contestable and mutable across time and space. The very idea that institutions are capable of definitive purposeful action is extremely controversial. But even if we assume that this condition can be verified, we should expect

---

[9] Miller (2007) names his theory "a causal theory of institutional corruption," thus stressing the causal contribution of institutional action to realization of institutional purposes.

an ample margin of (reasonable) disagreement regarding what an institution's purpose is or (even more so) should be.[10] To appreciate this point, consider how the political role of lobbies in such countries as the United States has changed the very understanding of the services rendered by elected politicians as well as the assessment of their actions while in office. The purpose of elected officials' uses of their powers of office has been redesigned, as they are allegedly expected to respond to the interests of the lobbies implicated in their election. This transformation entails a certain degree of uncertainty in assessing the officeholders' action with reference to both its defining purpose (which becomes an object of disagreement) and the outcomes expected by the different parties (which risk being quite divisive).

The identification of a shared *telos* for institutional action may be quite difficult and divisive for many complex institutions. For certain relatively simple institutions, we may follow Miller in the straightforward identification of the purpose of, say, a hospital with the provision of health care. True, the identification of what exactly pursuing the end of providing health care requires may be itself contentious because, for example, hospital management may be facing trade-offs with economic efficiency. But we should expect that the identification of such a purpose is even more controversial in the case of such complex entities as political institutions: Should parliaments pursue the common good, justice, or the public interest? What substantive interpretations of these ideas ought to give concrete directions to political-institutional action? An

---

[10] Reference to these margins of disagreement belongs to the standard "furniture" of liberal deontological critiques of teleological normative theories, especially when institutional purposes are defined in terms of some idea of the common or collective good (whose production justifies an institution instrumentally). Miller (2017, 69) seems to bite the bullet of this normative weakness when he writes: "A single instance of breach of fiduciary duty . . . might not undermine an institutional process or purpose. Moreover, whether such breaches tend to undermine institutional processes or purposes is a matter of contingent fact and not of logical necessity." See also Lessig (2018, 34–35). To bypass these uncertainties, we refer to an institution's functions (which might be multiple and changing over time) as constituting its raison d'être (see Chapters 1 and 2).

institutionalist may reply that these questions can be answered by presenting institutional purposes in terms of the officeholders' individual intentions. However, in the normal circumstances of politics characterized by (reasonable) disagreement, there seems to be no ground to expect that such a reductive strategy could solve the problem of determining a generally shared substantive interpretation of institutional purposes, thereby creating a cacophony of different views that could hardly sustain purposeful institutional action.

Consequentialist accounts aspire to offer a sizable criterion for assessing political corruption from an objective (consequence- or purpose-based) perspective. When this criterion is tainted with uncertainty and indeterminacy (and is open to disagreement), measurement of the negative exogenous or endogenous consequences of institutional action is difficult and their assessment debatable. The normative uncertainties that derive from these divisive questions may substantially undermine the capacity of consequentialist approaches to give solid guidance for the normative assessment of political corruption.[11]

Consequentialist assessments may still work facing macroscopic cases of political corruption (such as major cases of systemic bribery), whose negative consequences are sizable, largely predictable, and allegedly unequivocal against the background of a relatively simple institutional setting, whose purpose is not as controversial. But many cases of political corruption are far from being so straightforward. We have already encountered many such cases in our discussions so far; think once again of the appointment of Ivanka Trump and her husband, Jared Kushner, as advisors to the president of the United States (see Chapter 1). Or reconsider the intricacies of the corrupt system established around the construction works of the Berlin Willy Brandt Airport discussed in

---

[11] This limitation is acknowledged in deLeon (1993, 31–37) and Miller, Roberts, and Spence (2005, 67).

Chapter 2. Or revisit for a moment our case of familism in this chapter. Imagine, specifically, that Louise's decision to hire her husband, Matthew, solely to salvage her marriage does not happen to be unlawful, nor does it have any economic or sociopolitical costs, perhaps because Matthew turns out to be competent and no other candidate had applied for the position. Imagine also that Louise's action is just a one-off and that we can therefore expect it not to have any general negative implication for the institution's capacity to fulfill its purpose, and, therefore, not affect its integrity and trustworthiness. In these circumstances, adopting a consequentialist perspective (in any of its variants) may lead to the conclusion that Louise's conduct is not problematic or is even morally justified. But is this conclusion warranted? Can we really say that a politician who hires her husband as her chief of staff to salvage their marriage does nothing morally objectionable at all in the absence of any sizable negative effect?

A possible consequentialist rejoinder could come from distinguishing between act-based and rule-based forms of consequentialism. In view of this distinction, our qualms may be justified if targeted at act-consequentialism. However, from a rule-consequentialist perspective, we could consider the long-term foreseeable systemic effects of certain actions should they become a norm of conduct. So, while the wrongness of Louise's appointment of her husband might be discounted if taken as an isolated *act* and at face value, if familism became a *rule*, quite clear and foreseeable systemic negative consequences would follow. Familism, one could argue, *tends* to promote virtues other than professional competence and merit. Moreover, by approaching public office as a family matter, if Louise's conduct were the norm, it would reinforce people's political disaffection by corroborating the feeling that access to public office is the preserve of a few privileged people. Some of the qualms concerning Ms. Trump's and Mr. Kushner's appointments to the White House seem to make sense from this point of view.

Many objections have been leveled against the theoretical internal coherence of rule-consequentialism and its conceptual and normative independence from act-consequentialism.[12] Engaging with those objections would distract from our main line of argument in this chapter. We have no intention to reject a consequentialist assessment of political corruption altogether. We recognize that consequentialism (across its variants) captures *some* important sense of how political corruption is wrong. However, we also think that it cannot tell the whole story about the wrongness of political corruption on its own terms. We view this limitation as twofold. First, the consequences (of a corrupt act or norm) are inevitably exposed to the verification or plausibility of certain causal empirical exogenous or endogenous links, which are difficult to establish with certainty and might actually not hold at all. Second, any consequentialist reading draws on a comparative analysis of the costs (be they material or otherwise) that follow a certain action or norm with respect to both the benefits of such actions or norms and the cost-benefit balance of alternative actions or norms.

Suppose that Louise's familistic conduct were the norm and that, as a consequence, people would question the public nature of the institution in which she worked and access to the institution would be closed to people unrelated to some officeholders. But suppose also that, at the same time, they could see that, by recruiting family members, the institutional functioning would become more efficient because officeholders can communicate more effectively and make the most of their mutual connections on the basis of personal liaisons of trust. This is arguably the case for Kushner's appointment to the White House. Kushner's achievements include the 2018 criminal justice reform bill and the 2018–20 trade deal between the United States, Canada, and Mexico. In an interview with the *New York Times*, Kushner explained that, key to his achievements,

---

[12] For an overview, see Hooker (2015). We are grateful to Robert Sparling for encouraging us to address this perspective.

was the fact that "the President trusts me, and he knows I've had his back, and he knows that I've been able to execute for him on a lot of different objectives" (Bennett 2020). Appointing family members to positions of power in the U.S. government is not new in American history. Think of Robert F. Kennedy who was appointed attorney general during the Kennedy administration or Hillary Clinton's leading role in the health care reform initiative during her husband, Bill's administration. After examining these instances, can we be so sure that familism cannot be justified as a norm? What common currency could we have to assess the relative costs and benefits of the alternative rules of appointment and their consequences? Rule-consequentialism might identify certain *tendencies*, but the normative assessments it can deliver on its own seem to be erratic, by its own standards of objectivity, like those of act-consequentialism, though perhaps to a lesser degree. Their erratic nature depends on the cost-benefit comparative reasoning that any kind of consequentialism requires, which in the distinctively muddy circumstances of political corruption may expose the reasoning that should guide individual and institutional exercises of powers of office to some significant indeterminacy.

We can recognize the difficulties linked to such indeterminacy, for example, in the implementation of some current anticorruption policies in the context of redress and institution building in postwar scenarios. Recent evidence from the Democratic Republic of Congo, for example, shows that for ordinary Congolese citizens, the bribes paid by their fellow citizens do not have a negative connotation simply because they view this practice of corruption as the way to get basic social services and because they do not believe anticorruption measures can be effective anyway. However, they still have a negative attitude toward the corrupt conduct of public officeholders. This negative evaluation is mainly consequentialist, for it draws on the distributive injustices that political corruption produces. At the same time, citizens do not tend to punish corrupt politicians by voting them out of office; their voting behavior is largely determined by tribal belonging and the prospect of benefiting from the related relationships of clientele (UNDP 2010, 29–30).

The discussion thus far alerts us to the risks of addressing political corruption exclusively in terms of its negative consequences. The main risk is that such a perspective will discount the wrongness of political corruption in a way that will create incentives for corrupt behavior as one's most rational course of action to enhance one's opportunities and well-being. Especially in emergency situations, such as those ingenerated after an armed conflict, cost-benefit considerations may indicate both to local actors and to foreign aiders the advantages of corrupt exchanges in the distribution of resources, the balance of power among different parties, and the stabilization of political power. These are powerful deterrents that play against the development of anticorruption programs. These sorts of instrumental considerations exacerbate the legacy of war by perpetuating unjust societal relations that transfer within the new institutional setting and multiply the opportunities for corrupt action rather than undercutting them (see, e.g., Kodi 2008 and Le Billion 2003).

As will be seen in the next section, a deontological outlook on a public ethics of office should integrate the consequentialist logic common to many received approaches to date so as to offer a more determinate guidance for individual and institutional action.

3. The deontological assessment of political corruption as a relational wrong

In this section, we invite our readers to rethink the normative assessment of political corruption from a deontological perspective. With regard to institutional action, deontological theories differ from consequentialist theories because they do not focus on the normative properties of the states of affairs endogenously or exogenously caused by the action in question, but primarily on the normative properties inherent to the action itself. This deontological perspective helps us see the wrongness inherent in political corruption as a sui generis problem of public ethics, distinctive from and irreducible to the assessment of the negative consequences it does or is expected to bring about. To this end, we suggest revisiting the case of familism presented earlier by shifting the focus from the normative evaluation of the effects of the politician's use of her power of office to the features of her conduct in her institutional capacity. Our suggestion is that by hiring her husband, Matthew, as her chief of staff to salvage their marriage, Louise acts in an inherently wrongful way. The wrongness inherent in her conduct consists in a violation of the duty of office accountability that officeholders acquire when taking up their institutional functions. To concentrate on this violation is helpful to understand why the Trump–Kushner appointments to the White House were inherently problematic, aside from the practical advantages it gave to the realization of Donald Trump's presidential agenda.

To see what the duty of office accountability is and why it matters, recall from Chapter 1 the basic view of an institution as a system of interrelated embodied roles to which powers are entrusted with a mandate, established in keeping with an institution's raison d'être. Power mandates are normative in the sense of guiding the officeholders' actions: They establish what people acquire the right and the duty to do simply by occupying a certain role within an institution. The normative order thus created is constitutive of an institution and can only be seen and understood by looking at the officeholders' interrelated action in which the functioning of an institution consists.[13] We can thus appreciate

---

[13] In this sense, officeholders' actions are guided by what Applbaum (1999, 63–65) has called "role-relative moral prescriptions." For Emmet, a "role is a capacity in which someone acts in relation to others" (1966, 13); "in a role one is a person of a certain kind put in a certain kind of relationship, and thus detached from purely personal idiosyncrasy" (Emmet 1966, 158). For a discussion of human action in an institutional capacity from an alternative teleological perspective, see Miller (2017, 33).

how a well-functioning institution is premised on the division of labor between officeholders: Institutional roles are interrelated in a way that makes the functioning of the institution dependent (by virtue of the many mechanisms expounded in Chapter 2) on every officeholder's performing his or her functions in keeping with their mandates. The functioning of an institution structurally depends on the officeholders' capacity to act on their rights and duties of office, which depend in turn on the other officeholders' performance of their respective rights and duties as detailed by their power mandates. This normative order thus establishes officeholders with the *authority* to hold one another accountable for the uses they make of their powers of office when they act in their institutional capacity. This is the idea of *office accountability*, the structural property of well-functioning institutions introduced in Chapter 1. Office accountability governs the institutional role-based relations between officeholders, who should always be in the position to give each other an account of the rationale of the agenda that underpins how they use their power of office and show its coherence with the terms of their power mandate.[14] The mutual moral authority to claim this kind of account against each other correlates with a moral duty for every officeholder always to put herself in that position when she acts in her institutional capacity; this is the duty of office accountability.

The duty of office accountability is a special moral duty of institutional membership, which derives from the normative status people acquire as participants in an interrelated structure of institutional roles. When they act and interact in their institutional capacity, officeholders' rights and duties are not determined solely by

[14] The terms of a power mandate thus provide the common knowledge base that should inform any exercise of power and the justification thereof. For a Kant-inspired reading of this idea, see Luban (2012). For a similar relational view of accountability in the domain of personal (rather than institutional) moral relations, see Korsgaard (1996). And for a general statement of the claim that interpersonal moral relations fundamentally occur in terms of mutual accountability, which establish people as second-personal authorities, see Darwall (2006).

the law or the principles of personal ethics (such as the harm principle). Their conduct is also shaped and limited by a special body of moral norms binding on an individual qua the occupant of an institutional role. As officeholders, people acquire a role-specific set of obligations, which are morally binding on them as a consequence of their voluntary decision to enter a certain office.[15] The normative force of those obligations may be corroborated by their being instrumental to an institution's capacity to deliver certain valuable goods. But the officeholders also have reasons to abide by their role-based obligations that are internal to the relations they entertain with each other.[16] This is to say that institutions as a system of role-based interactions generate an internal kind of relational normativity that is not reducible to the normativity of the separate acts individual officeholders are expected (legally or morally) to perform. The new possibility for actions created by establishing institutional role-based relations depends on a structure of rights and duties that demands support by each officeholder as interrelated with every other.[17] The participation in the normative order constituted by these role-based interactions gives

[15] John Simmons (1979, 19) explains how voluntariness can make positional duties morally binding even if they are not perfect duties as those that can be enforced by a code of conduct. He illustrates this viewpoint by referring to the case of the president of the United States failing to fulfill his positional duties, which makes him not only legally but also morally blameworthy because he voluntarily undertook to perform the duties of that position. Voluntariness per se cannot generate morally binding institutional duties when the background conditions for taking up an institutional role are deeply unjust. As Simmons notes, it is highly questionable whether the voluntary acceptance of duties under the Nazi regime could have generated morally binding obligations. We discuss the relevance of this example later on in this chapter with reference to the normative force of the duty of office accountability outside the context of legitimate of nearly just institutions (§4).

[16] Mokrosinska (2012) uses the expression "value internal to relations" to qualify a kind of normativity that supervenes on the relations created with the inauguration of human forms of interaction.

[17] Hart (1955), Rawls (1971), and Klosko (1992) argue that certain considerations of fair-play offer the moral ground to positional duties. As participants in a cooperative scheme, officeholders acquire particular obligations linked to their position. The reasoning structure of these arguments is analogous to the one we follow to elucidate the normativity of the duty of office accountability (whereas we do not think institutions may be reduced to cooperative instruments for the production of certain goods).

officeholders moral reasons to demand of each other compliance with their duties of office.

So, a teacher's duty to assess her students' performance impartially (regardless of her personal sympathies or the prestige of the students' families) is not just a matter of honoring either a voluntary contracted professional obligation, or a general moral commitment to fair treatment, nor is it just grounded in the instrumental value of this line of conduct in view of the educational purposes of the schooling system. The normative source of this duty is in the normative order of role-based relations within which her action acquires a sense as it is considered in the interrelation with that of her fellow members. These are the role-based relations that the teacher entertains with the other teachers who teach to that class, but also with the school staff, e.g., the administrators. The performance of the teacher's functions (the exercise of their rights and duties) depends on the teacher's acting according to a rationale that is coherent with the terms of the power mandate that defines her role—which certainly do not include the expression of the teacher's idiosyncrasies or the enticement of potential school donors. In this sense, the duty of office accountability belongs to a relational public ethics of office. Officeholders directly owe the fulfillment of this duty to each other, and not merely to a third-person authority in virtue of their normative structural relations when they act in their institutional capacity.

Because we have characterized political corruption as a deficit of office accountability, we can now assess its wrongness as a violation of the corresponding duty of office. From this vantage point, when Louise hires Matthew as her chief of staff to salvage their marriage, she makes a wrongful use of her power of office for the pursuit of an agenda alien to the terms of the mandate that governs the role that gives her the power to act in that very instance. Therefore, she is not in the position to respond to the claim of accounting for the rationale of her conduct as coherent with the terms of her power mandate. In this sense, Louise's conduct signposts a specific kind of wrongdoing that consists in an alteration of the relational patterns between officeholders. Her action is thus inherently wrong because it instantiates (does not merely cause) a failure of the normative order of interactions constitutive of an institution.

Of course, real-life cases are hardly as linear to assess. However, the adoption of our proposed perspective offers a fresh lens for reexamining the wrongness of the appointment of Ivanka Trump and her husband as White House advisors. This assessment is not limited to the consequences of these appointments but also concerns the net of relations constituted by the access the protagonists of this affair have gained to an office headed by a close family member. These relations involve father, daughter, and son-in-law, as well as the other members of the Trump administration. These relations are constituted by the very exercise of the power of appointment. The whole normative order of these institutional relations is at risk, as it is strained by a dual logic that muddles the personal with the institutional. This strain is particularly evident, for example, in the uneasiness manifested anytime Ms. Trump was asked to comment on her father's implication in alleged sexual harassment scandals or episodes of misogyny. [18]

The inherent wrongness of political corruption can be further illuminated through the lens of interactive justice.[19] Generally speaking, interactive justice is a normative property of interpersonal relations; it concerns the kind of treatment that people owe to each other in their deontic interactions (Ceva 2016, 5–7, 50). That is to say, an interactive injustice occurs when someone is not given the kind of treatment owed to her in virtue of her normative status. Interactive justice is, therefore, a relational kind of justice, the idea that "when people stand in a certain relationship to one another,

---

[18] Interviewed by NBC on the subject, Ms. Trump is reported to have said that she thinks "it's a pretty inappropriate question to ask a daughter if she believes the accusers of her father, when he's affirmatively stated there's no truth to that, . . . I don't think that's a question you would ask many other daughters" (Parker and Rucker 2018).

[19] For the idea of interactive justice, see Ceva (2016, Ch. 1).

they become subject to principles of justice whose scope is limited to those within the relationship" (D. Miller 2017). Interactive injustice is neither the expected nor the actual consequence of establishing such interactions; an interactively unjust practice or behavior is inherently wrong because it is constitutive of someone's wrongful treatment.

On the basis of this characterization of interactive justice, the duty of office accountability can be explained as a duty of interactive justice (because it qualifies the deontic relations between officeholders) and, conversely, political corruption as a form of interactive injustice (because it qualifies a failure of those relations and the normative order they instantiate).[20] Violations of the duty of office accountability do not materialize when officeholders fail to answer ex post for the consequences of their conduct in their institutional capacity. The duty of office accountability is the primary component of a public ethics of office, and as such it has a regulative power over the officeholders' conduct. Violations of this duty may thus occur even in the absence of concrete answerability measures and procedures.[21] In this light, Louise's duty is not solely to answer retrospectively for the (actual or expected) consequences of the corrupt exercise of her power of appointment.[22] She also has the prospective duty to consider her institutional action as limited by the constraints of her power mandate, which commands, inter alia, that considerations concerning her spousal relation to Matthew be excluded from the practical reasoning that guides the exercise of

---

[20] Bovens et al. (2014, 4) recognize this "relational and communicative core" as one of the main components of the conceptual consensus in the scholarly debate on accountability.

[21] Along these lines, see Bovens's distinction between accountability as a virtue and accountability as a mechanism (Bovens 2010).

[22] Kolstad (2012) has presented consequentialist as well as deontological reasons to view the wrongness of political corruption as the violation of the "distributed obligations" associated with role-related uses of entrusted powers of office. While our view is germane to Kolstad's, it offers a more specific and refined argument as it introduces a novel *deontological* assessment of the wrongness of political corruption as a form of "interactive injustice."

her power of office. Because Louise's action, as an instance of political corruption, fails this duty, we can see that it is inherently wrong because it is constitutive of an interactively unjust institutional dynamic. Louise's conduct is inherently wrong because it violates a moral duty of public ethics.

More generally, consider clientelism, the practice by which a certain group of citizens has access to benefits because of their special relation as "clients" of their public "patrons." Clients enjoy a "fast track" to make their claims reach the political agenda, influence decision making, and affect rule-implementation. The access to such a track is reserved to clients owing to their special personal relation with their patrons. Therefore, the uses patrons make of their power of office fails office accountability. We can now see how this use of power is inherently wrong, as it constitutes a kind of relation (of clientelism, or nepotism and familism as in the previous examples) that fails the normative order of the interactions between officeholders within a public institution. The inherent injustice of these forms of interaction is retained even when the benefits of a corrupt relation spill over and extend to third parties or when their negative actual or foreseeable consequences are not clearly assessable.

By offering this account of the interactive injustice of political corruption, we do not mean to trivialize the moral importance of the negative consequences to which political corruption may lead. Our intention is, rather, to suggest an overarching account of why we should also look at political corruption as an injustice in its own terms. This account is general and fundamental, for it consists in the violation of a general and fundamental duty of office that is structurally binding on all officeholders. Violations of the duty of office accountability are at the core of our normative discussion of political corruption because they are a basic failure of the normative order of interactions constitutive of a public institution, In this sense, we can reinforce our claim that political corruption—as a problem of public ethics—is an *internal* enemy of public institutions.

So far, we have illustrated our office-accountability-based normative perspective on political corruption with reference to cases of individual corrupt conduct in the form of familism, nepotism, or clientelism. In view of our continuity thesis, we can also claim that adopting this perspective may shed new light on cases in which, in virtue of the interrelatedness of institutional roles, political corruption can be predicated on entire institutional practices. To see this further aspect, reconsider one of the most representative cases in the institutionalist orthodoxy, the case of the "Keating Five." In the late 1980s, as a result of a series of high-risk investments, Charles H. Keating's company, Lincoln Savings and Loan, collapsed, thus causing a large number of uninsured customers to lose their savings. In the course of the investigations of Keating's company, five U.S. senators whose electoral campaigns Keating had financed engaged in a series of meetings with different authorities for the regulation of industry to inquire into the status of Keating's position. During these meetings, the Keating Five pressured for the investigations to be speeded up, which would thereby accrue to Keating's advantage.

In his discussion of the Keating Five case, Thompson (1993) maintained that to understand the *political* wrongness of the case, we must view it as an instantiation of the broader institutional practice of private financing and consider the damage that this institutionalized practice caused to democratic government. From this institutionalist perspective, what matters politically is not the personal gain produced by the corrupt exchange. Rather, attention should be paid to the political advantage that is thereby created.[23] This advantage does not serve the public officials' personal interests. Instead, it accrues to the officials in the performance of their public functions. In the Keating case, it consisted in the electoral mandate

---

[23] For a similar discussion of corruption in the U.S. Congress, see Lessig (2018, Ch. 1).

the senators obtained through Keating's generous contributions to their campaigns.

Looking at this case only in terms of the dichotomy between the individual corruption of the senators' personal motives, on the one hand, and the institutional corruption of the practice of private campaign financing and its distorting effects, on the other, does not capture all the complexities of the structural relations at work. We recognize the dangers of the institutional mechanism of power acquisition that distorts the dynamics of power exercise. But to understand how these exercises of power are wrong, we must look at the structural relations between the officeholders— the senators and Keating as a citizen and a funder of the senators' electoral campaign—and study their logic. We can thus see that the five senators' institutional actions were interactively unjust; what was wrong in the relations they entertained was their violation of their duty of office accountability when they used their power of office to inquire about the state of the investigation of Keating's company in order to accelerate the proceedings. By this reading, we do not lose sight of what the institutionalists are mainly concerned about, but we can also bring into focus the relational dynamics by which political corruption erodes an institution from the inside as the sources and sites of its wrongness. As Chapters 4 and 5 illustrate, this structural-relational reading of the wrongness of political corruption in institutional practices as an interactive injustice has important implications for the capacity to assign responsibilities for corruption and anticorruption within a public institution as a matter of a public ethics of office accountability.

We can thus see how the corrupt conduct of public officials and corrupt institutional practices are presumptively wrong in themselves as a problem of public ethics. This is an important conclusion of our argument. But more work is still necessary to qualify the scope of the normative judgments that can thus be issued. Are these judgments of political corruption absolute and unconditional?

That is to say, is political corruption always and necessarily wrong, all things considered?

4. The scope of the interactive injustice of political corruption

We have argued that political corruption constitutes an interactive injustice because it is a violation of the duty of office accountability. In this section, we establish the scope of this argument by considering the circumstances that may (1) undermine the cogency of the assessment of the wrongness of political corruption and make its wrongness either (2) pro tanto (and therefore excusable, all things considered) or (3) prima facie (and therefore justified).

The basic circumstance to consider in this regard is that, as expounded in Chapter 1, any use of an entrusted power may be the object of some (reasonable) disagreement as concerns both the content of that power mandate and the terms of its exercise. This circumstance of disagreement is generally true but is particularly the case for uses of the powers of office, given the inevitable margins of discretion standardly associated with institutional roles.[24] This disagreement may undermine the cogency of our normative assessment of political corruption as it concerns the very term of reference used to test accountability. This threat is worrisome because as we have seen, a crucial element of our argument is to offer guidance for the assessment of political corruption that is more cogent than that offered by consequentialist approaches (exposed to the uncertainty of the outcomes of a comparative cost-benefit analysis of the consequences of this phenomenon).

In fact, the likelihood of such disagreements may make the advantage of looking at political corruption as a matter of public ethics grounded in a duty of office accountability even more

---

[24] For a discussion, see, for example, Applbaum (1992).

significant. To appreciate this significance, we must look at the conceptual, factual, and normative link between discretion and accountability. Consider that discretion "is not 'doing as one pleases' within the bounds of the law. The official must be able to *explain* on what grounds he or she selected a particular alternative among the many that were available" (Zacka 2017, 34; emphasis added).To say that officeholders have a duty of office accountability means, primarily, that they must always act in such a way that allows them to offer such an explanation with reference to the terms of their power mandate, so as to fend off possible disagreements as concerns their exercise of their powers of office. This duty requires, first and foremost, showing that their exercise of power is coherent with either the spirit or the letter of their mandate. But it may also require that, should the letter (the content) of the mandate be unclear or contested, they can vindicate their conduct with reference to the spirit of their mandate. When they cannot do so, their conduct becomes corrupt and interactively unjust. The relational nature of the duty of office accountability suggests the dialogical, communicative nature of the principle that should guide an officeholder's conduct.

The idea of accountability at the core of a public ethics of office is thus meant to offer an internal intersubjective perspective grounded in the interrelatedness of institutional roles. From this perspective, officeholders are called to engage critically with their conduct. This is an important innovative feature of our argument that we will develop in the next chapter as regards the attribution of responsibilities for corruption and anticorruption. For the time being, this feature allows us to see why the disagreement that concerns the terms of an officeholder's power mandate is not as damaging to our argument as the indeterminacy of institutional purposes and the uncertainty of the consequences of institutional action are for the consequentialist approaches we reviewed in the previous section. We have seen that the plausibility of these views importantly depends on the reliance on a measurable criterion for assessing institutional action (by assessing its results) from both inside and outside an institution. Our office accountability view stresses instead the need for an internal perspective on political corruption and its assessment by drawing on an institution's capacity for self-scrutiny and self-correction, which requires (and thrives on) the dialogical engagement of officeholders with any uncertainty as concerns the definition and use of their power mandate.

Here we need to clarify the relation between our proposed deontological assessment of political corruption as an interactive injustice and another, consequentialist sense in which this form of corruption may be deemed unjust: as a source of "end-state" injustices. From the perspective of end-state justice, a politically corrupt conduct or institutional practice is unjust to the extent that it has some negative consequences on the distributive patterns of people's subjective moral rights (see, e.g., Miller, Roberts, and Spence 2005, 63–4). For example, patronage may entail an unequal distribution of people's rights to fair job opportunities; bribery may infringe upon rights to fair play; and vote buying may hinder the distribution of citizens' rights to democratic participation. These considerations instantiate in the moral domain the teleological reasoning we discussed earlier in this chapter.

The view of political corruption as a form of end-state injustice yields some important insights concerning how political corruption is unjust. However, in light of our argument in the previous section, this view cannot tell the whole story about the wrongness of political corruption because, like any other form of consequentialism, it is burdened by some significant uncertainties whenever political corruption does not result in clear and sizable (actual or expected) distributive injustices.

With this view in mind, let us revisit Louise's hiring of her husband, Matthew. One possible account that explains why Louise's corrupt use of her power of office is wrong consists in arguing that Matthew's appointment, regardless of his qualifications, implies a form of partiality that violates the equal employment opportunities of the other candidates. In this sense, we could say that this episode of political corruption is unjust because it is causally related to a distributive injustice concerning the other candidates' moral rights. But what if it turns out that the other applicants are not any better qualified than Louise's husband? Or what if Matthew is the only candidate for that job? In these potential scenarios, it appears much less obvious that Louise's corrupt use of her power of office has been partial in a way that has caused any alteration of the distributive patterns of anyone's subjective rights. Of course one could say that, from the perspective of rule-consequentialism, there are ampler margins to argue that the distributive patterns of people's rights to equal employment opportunities in the public sector would be foreseeably undermined were Louise's conduct the norm. Besides the critical considerations we introduced earlier concerning the cogency of this approach, we want to emphasize that *even if* this consequentialist argument worked, it would nevertheless miss an important general and constitutive aspect of the wrongness of Louise's conduct.

In each of these scenarios, Louise's conduct is (and does not merely entail) an interactive injustice, which consists in her violation of her duty of office accountability. Her commitment to salvaging her spousal relation by using her power of office to appoint Matthew as her chief of staff is plainly not an agenda whose rationale can possibly be vindicated as coherent with the terms of her power mandate. Of course, this familial logic could be less objectionable if the hiring processes were situated in a family-owned business. But it is clear that, within the context of a public institution, Louise's conduct is unjust—generally and consistently—in our terms. Were Louise to justify her choice, she would be forced to redescribe the agenda that underpins her use of power by reinventing its rationale in ways that cohere with the mandate that ought to regulate her action in her institutional capacity (e.g., by referring to a general idea of trust that—she could say—informs the spirit of her mandate to select a right-hand man on whom she could blindly rely). This redescription flags a deficit of office accountability and, therefore, a failure of the normative order constitutive of the institution where Louise (and Matthew) operate. This failure is not a consequence of political corruption, to which corrupt acts are either exogenously or endogenously causally related; it is, rather, a structural feature of any corrupt use of a power of office.

A similar line of reasoning applies to those cases in which an instance of political corruption has allegedly distributive-justice-enhancing consequences. Think, for example, of a country where political action is hampered by governmental bottlenecks based on conservative relations of clientele that stand in the way of progressive policies aimed at enhancing citizens' welfare. In these contexts, political corruption such as bribery—even if carried out in the exclusive interest of the corrupt parties—may have the (probably unintended) effect of benefiting the collectivity when they lead, say, to the building of a hospital or other infrastructure that would otherwise not be built. This is arguably the situation in one of the major recent cases of corruption in China which implicated Bo Xilai, a party secretary of Chongqind, who transformed his inland city with new roads, hospitals, and housing infrastructure through foreign investments gained through a reckless, debt-fueled construction policy.[25] Our deontological assessment of political corruption can give strong reasons not to let these cases of political corruption off the hook. It provides the normative resources to assess the wrongness of political corruption independently of the uncertainties that derive from a cost-benefit comparative analysis of the actual or expected consequences of bribery (either as an act or a rule).

Notice another interesting implication of this argument. The allegedly positive consequences of political corruption in terms of end-state justice can be seen as a symptom of an underlying, deeper

---

[25] For a discussion of corruption within the context of Chinese economic expansion, see Ang (2020). We examine the so-called Chinese paradox toward the end of this chapter.

form of injustice. Differently put, in nonideal conditions, in which distributive principles of end-state justice are disregarded, the allegedly positive distributive effects of such interactively unjust actions as episodes of political corruption may have the heuristic function of suggesting the presence of an underlying injustice to which political corruption is an adaptive response. This consideration shows that the concrete links between interactive and end-state justice might be quite complicated to disentangle and assess in such nonideal circumstances as those of political corruption. But this exercise is necessary to gain an overall understanding of the mechanisms of political corruption within a public institution and their wrongness.

Notably, when the two normative judgments of end-state and interactive injustice coincide, we can say that an episode of political corruption is wrong, all things considered. An illustration of this coincidence comes from cases of systemic bribery in countries dominated by an oligarchy. Systemic bribery can be seen as wrong both inherently (because of the interactive injustice that characterizes the oligarchs' violation of their duty of office accountability) and in light of its negative consequences (such as the end-state injustice of the resulting impoverishment of the weaker parts of the population). When only one of the two dimensions of injustice is verified, we can say that an episode of political corruption is pro tanto wrong because neither of the two dimensions may discount on its own the wrongness of the other. This refined understanding of the wrongness of political corruption is not only analytically important, but, as we will see in the next chapters, it also has significant implications for assigning responsibilities for corruption and anticorruption.

With the introduction of the qualification that, in certain institutional circumstances, the wrongness of political corruption may be pro tanto, we have reached a further important normative point of our argument. To see this point, consider that sometimes the challenge to the assessment of the wrongness of political corruption may run even deeper than what we could appreciate in our discussion so far. These are times when the disagreement concerns the spirit as well as the letter of a power mandate. By acknowledging the earlier-mentioned heuristic function of political corruption, we can see that, in some institutional circumstances, the presence of political corruption may indicate that a certain power mandate is either very controversial or radically contested. In these circumstances, political corruption may have the heuristic function of bringing to the fore concerns about the very justice or legitimacy of a mandate or, in fact, of the institutional system in which that mandate is entrusted to an institutional role. In such cases, the wrongness of political corruption could be excused (qua pro tanto) or in fact fully discounted (qua prima facie).

To start from the most radical claim, consider the case of Oskar Schindler, a German businessman and a member of the Nazi Party, who bribed Nazi officials to rescue Jews from concentration camps by hiring them as factory workers. This case may go under the heading of "noble-cause corruption" (see, e.g., Miller 2017, 89–103). While these cases can be categorized under the *descriptive* heading of political corruption (in keeping with our argument in Chapter 1), their *normative* evaluation is not as straightforward. To give a complete, all-things-considered, normative assessment of these forms of corruption, we cannot and should not disregard the background injustice of the institutional circumstances when the relevant use of power occurs. In these circumstances, Schindler's bribe can be seen as an act of resistance, with the heuristic capacity of revealing an unjust institutional system.[26]

The corrupt action works as a sort of alarm bell in contexts where some wrongdoing is normalized. True, in such circumstances the single instance of political corruption may easily go unnoticed; in fact, sometimes, in order to be functional to its own ends, it must be

---

[26] We have discussed this case in previous work under the heading of "civil disobedience" (see Ceva and Ferretti 2018, 226–27).

kept secret. Moreover, it is exactly because such acts are not immediately recognized as a form of resistance that they can be dubbed
as corruption or treason. But when we analyze these cases with the
benefit of hindsight, we can appreciate why to call them "corrupt"
does not straightforwardly entail their moral condemnation. The
all-things-considered assessment of such cases should include both
a reflection on the end-state justice that such corrupt exchanges
as that between Schindler and the Nazi officers entails (in terms
of protecting people's fundamental rights) *and* the interactive injustice of their violation of the duty of office accountability. Cases
like this one allow us to see that, in certain unjust or illegitimate
institutional circumstances, political corruption can be justified
both because it yields end-state justice *and* it is only prima facie interactively unjust. The duty of office accountability, which is generally binding on officeholders, loses its normative force when its
violations reveal the deeper injustice of the very terms of the mandate and the normative order that the corrupt officeholder fails by
her action.[27]

These considerations show the importance of the heuristic function of political corruption and also prompt a general remark concerning the general underlying logic of its normative assessment.
It is a fundamental tenet of this book that we should be wary of
referring to political corruption as a "catch-all" category for making
sense of any kind of institutional wrong or malfunctioning. The
many common but figurative uses of the term suggest that this tendency is quite widespread in both the scholarly and public debate
as it is used to indicate such diverse mechanisms as state capture,
fraud, or even "revolving door" practices in a democracy. This book
makes a distinctive case against such a tendency to be overinclusive.
The many figurative uses of "political corruption" are problematic

---

[27] For a discussion of how an obligation does not establish an absolute moral claim on
a subject's action, see Simmons (1979, 19); and for a justification of why the Nazi official
cannot be morally bounded by the duties of his office, see Simmons (1979, 18).

for the study of institutional dysfunctions both in analytical and normative terms. By overstretching the concept of political corruption, the risk is failing to grasp its distinctive dynamics and the salience of its wrongness. This risk emerges whenever references to political corruption are made to assess the general moral character of a whole institutional structure (like the Nazi regime in our example). Surely, political corruption has in some cases the heuristic function of revealing underlying injustices at the institutional level. In other cases, it may well be that systemic corrupt uses of powers of office may end up causally undermining the overall justice (or legitimacy) of an entire institutional system. But the most significant problem in such cases is that there is an unjust (or illegitimate) institutional system. Corruption should not be used as either the name or the reductivist basis of any form of institutional wrongdoing.

To bring political corruption into focus as an object of public ethics on its own terms means to look at this phenomenon as a specific instance of institutional wrongdoing. This gives us the tools for understanding and assessing the interrelated uses that officeholders make of their powers of office within public institutions that might be otherwise well designed. To consider political corruption (not only its more or less systemic consequences) as an object of public ethics is thus necessary to identify a specific sense in which political corruption is an internal enemy of public institutions.

Another set of problems worthy of discussion comes from the "dirty hands" debate. These problems emerge from the tragic choices between morally wrong courses of action that an officeholder is likely to face as the "stuff" of political action, even within legitimate or generally just institutional settings.[28] The choice can be either between personal and public values (e.g., sacrificing the interests of some close ones for the benefit of the community) or

---

[28] This is the view presented in Walzer (1973). For a lengthy discussion, see Mendus (2009).

between different public values (e.g., individual rights and public security). The former instance raises issues of conscience, whereas the latter indicates conflicts within the domain of public ethics. Problems of dirty hands of the latter kind are particularly relevant for the discussion of political corruption: In cases of medical emergency, should a humanitarian NGO pay the customs official a bribe to facilitate the transit of drugs that would otherwise be obstructed? Inaction in such instances seems morally impossible, but any course of action that is undertaken brings with it a significant moral loss. While our account would thus join many others in the domain of political philosophy to acknowledge this kind of dilemma,[29] it may clarify the scenario by identifying the values to trade against each other in the common currency of justice. The interactive justice that would be secured by resisting corruption is in tension with the end-state justice that giving in to corruption would (most likely) realize. So we could say that, in these circumstances, political corruption is pro tanto wrong as an interactive injustice but could be all-things-considered excused in consideration of weighty countervailing considerations of end-state justice. These evaluations are principled and draw entirely on considerations of justice. They thus articulate a normative approach to political corruption that may not be reduced to a consequentialist comparative assessment of the expected outcomes of competing courses of action.

We can say something more about those uses of entrusted power of office that occur within a legitimate or generally (or else, "nearly") just institutional framework. Consider another common case of dirty hands that often comes to mind as an instance of

---

[29] Besides the classic Walzer (1973), see also Bellamy (2010). The question of whether and when an officeholder is justified in following her own judgment (irrespective of her role obligations) is also discussed in Applbaum (1992). For a recent discussion of the conflicts of duties that threaten the moral agency of "street-level" bureaucrats, see Zacka (2017).

noble-cause corruption: a police officer who fabricates evidence in the pursuit of justice—for example, to convict a drug lord.[30] To the extent that the officer's use of his power of office occurs against the framework of generally legitimate or just institutions, we can appropriately describe the case as one of political corruption *but also* make normative sense of its pro tanto wrongness in terms of interactive injustice. The police officer can be seen as acting in violation of his duty of office accountability as he sidesteps the constraints that normally apply to his power mandate under the rule of law. Therefore, his corrupt conduct is inherently, albeit pro tanto, wrong whatever the ends it may have intended to further. Depending on the circumstances, the all-things-considered judgment of the police officer's conduct should also consider these ends. For example, it should include evaluation of the specific rules that govern the police modus operandi. The corrupt use of the police officer's power of office can be seen as instrumental to bypassing the inadequacy of these rules. From our deontological perspective, this consideration is by no means sufficient to call the corrupt officer's use of his power morally right; but it may show how it is all-things-considered excusable.

This twofold descriptive and normative discussion of political corruption represents a significant competitive advantage, as it were and inter alia, of our view with respect to other recent philosophical discussions that blur this line of separation by offering a normatively laden definition of this phenomenon. Let us see how.

---

[30] For a discussion of this case from the teleological perspective of institutional corruption, see Miller (2017, 90 ff.). In the debate about dirty hands, this case is referred to as that of "Dirty Harry"; for example, see Klockars (1980).

5. Impartiality, democratic equality, and office accountability

The crux of the argument we have developed in this chapter is a normative account of political corruption in the negative: a violation of what fulfilling the duty of office accountability requires of an officeholder who acts in her institutional capacity. But our argument also has a positive side, which concerns explaining why realizing office accountability in public institutions matters. To see the significance of office accountability it is also important to understand the advantages of our normative account of the wrongness of political corruption with respect to other recent principled normative approaches, which revolve around the ideas of impartiality and democratic equality.

A first contender in our office-accountability-based normative view revolves around the principle of impartiality, the idea that justice requires that a state "treat equally those who deserve equally" (see Rothstein and Varraich 2017, 55; Kurer 2005, 223; see also Rothstein and Teorell 2008). Although it offers a principled normative assessment of political corruption, the impartiality-based view grounds this assessment on consequentialist considerations of end-state justice. Political corruption is wrong because it violates the principle of impartiality; any such violation is morally problematic to the extent that it entails a violation of the subjective right against discrimination. For Bo Rothstein and Aiysha Varraich (2017, 58), this right is a human right, and its violation is wrong in view of its "costs in overall human well-being." For Oskar Kurer (2005, 227), we have a normatively problematic case of corruption when an officeholder violates "non-discrimination norms in order to gain a private advantage."

To illustrate the causal nexus between corruption and the violation of human rights, Rothstein and Varraich, for example, refer to those cases in which people end up paying for having access to certain public services that they are, in fact, entitled to receive as a matter of right because such services are central to human well-being. The examples they provide concern access to health care and education but also "personalized bureaucracies, situations where one's connections land one a job instead of one's merit" (Rothstein and Varraich 2017, 61). The common core of all these cases is a kind of injustice that consists in a violation of the basic human right against discrimination. This kind of injustice as discrimination is a property of the end-states generated by such corrupt exchanges as those that occur between the parties involved in practices of clientelism, patrimonialism, patronage, and state capture. For Rothstein and Varraich, the common feature that runs across these cases is a discriminatory use of public power that entails unacceptable human costs (Rothstein and Varraich 2017, 70 ff.).

There is much to say to pinpoint the affinities between our normative account of political corruption and that based on impartiality. These affinities concern the interest in identifying the *injustice* of political corruption, locating this injustice in certain unjustifiable uses of a *power* of office, and, therefore, viewing the problematic core of political corruption as ultimately concerning an *officeholder's conduct*. However, some important differences obtain too, most notably as concerns our interpretation of the injustice of political corruption (in terms of *interactive injustice*), the specific referent of what makes certain uses of power of office unaccountable (the *power mandate*), and, consequently, the assessment of the wrongness of individual officeholders' conduct, which we have presented in *deontological* terms rather than considering the end-state injustices deriving from the endogenous or exogenous consequences of institutional action.

We have already registered our qualms about normative views centered on a consequentialist focus, which also apply to approaches based on end-state injustice. These qualms primarily concern the erratic evaluations of the wrongness of political corruption to the extent that they depend on the verification of its causal empirical nexus with the (actual or foreseeable) occurrence

of such negative consequences as the violation of someone's subjective rights. Rothstein and Varraich faced the worrisome
implications of this limitation, for example, when they addressed
the so-called Chinese paradox: If political corruption is problematic because of the human costs that impartiality-defective uses of
public power entail, how can we make sense of this normative judgment in such seemingly successful cases of well-being-enhancing
growth (as that of China), where the corrupt administration has
entailed no economic setback (Rothstein and Varraich 2017, 103
ff.)? To make sense of this "puzzle," Rothstein and Varraich (2017,
113 ff., 121 ff.) are at pains to develop an articulated account of a
"cadre" administrative model whereby public power is exercised
in a sui generis impartial manner as an alternative to the Western
standards of the rule of law. Our view offers a simpler but no less cogent account capable of dissolving the Chinese paradox. From our
deontological point of view, there simply is no normative puzzle
at all. Insofar as some uses of a power of office occur for the pursuit of an agenda whose rationale is incoherent with the terms of
that power mandate, we can call that use of power "corrupt." This
labeling is sufficient to issue a pro tanto normative evaluation of
the wrongness of corrupt officeholders' actions or institutional
practices as constituting an interactive injustice within otherwise
well-designed public institutions. This evaluation is independent of
the (actual or foreseeable) consequences of this exercise of power.
Most notably, it does not entail an all-things-considered judgment
of the injustice of political corruption, which also includes the perspective of end-state justice and may run counter to a positive ap-
praisal of the distributive consequences of this phenomenon (e.g.,
as concerns human well-being).

Our points of disagreement with the impartiality-based view run
even deeper. First, this view overreaches because not all breaches
of the principle of impartiality are corrupt; they can in fact be due
to either a malicious discriminatory intent or carelessness. Second,
the impartiality-based account risks underreaching too because

not all instances of political corruption are problematic to the extent that they entail a breach of impartiality. To understand this point, consider the strict formulation of the impartiality-based model of "good governance" offered by Rothstein and Varraich (2017, 136): "When implementing laws and policies government officials shall not take anything into consideration about the citizen/case that is not beforehand stipulated in the policy or the law." This formulation corresponds to what we have characterized as uses of powers of office coherent with the letter of a power mandate. But, as we discussed at length in Chapter 1, there are two "buts." For a starter, certain uses of powers of office may be coherent with the *letter* of the mandate but violate its *spirit*. To identify the scope of an officeholder's justified action with whatever the letter of existing regulations happens to prescribe seems unnecessarily narrow. What is more, powers of office come with *discretion* and must be exercised sometimes with reference to laws and policies whose letter is far from clear and, thus, allows for margins of interpretation. This consideration suggests that the boundaries of the impartial use of a power of office are not as universal and clear-cut as Rothstein and Varraich (but also Kurer) present it.[31] Facing these uncertainties, our account has the resources to argue that (whatever the details of the law or policy to implement) public officials are under a duty of public ethics to use their power of office in ways that can withstand the scrutiny of office accountability. This duty also applies to employing the discretion that comes with their power and with its partial or impartial use. This is the essence of the duty of office accountability that corrupt uses of powers of office, as seen, constitutively violate.

[31] Sparling (2017) offers a similar critique when he argues that the impartiality-based approach to corruption risks depoliticizing the discussion of this phenomenon in a troublesome sense. Sparling (2017, 11–12) engages critically along these lines, also with a previous formulation of our argument, which he deems too inflexible in its commitment to impartiality (Ceva and Ferretti 2014). We hope that we have said enough to qualify our office-accountability-based view and, thus, take distance from the impartiality-based interpretation that Sparling has attributed to our normative stance.

Third, and finally, by offering a normatively laden definition of corruption,[32] the impartiality-based approach fails to capture the nuances of the normative judgments of this phenomenon that our account allows. While for us any use of a power of office in order to pursue an agenda whose rationale is not coherent with that power mandate can be described as corrupt, it is not necessarily wrong all things considered, although it constitutes a pro tanto interactive injustice that occurs against the background of otherwise well-designed public institutions. Moreover, as seen in the case of the seeming Chinese paradox, the impartiality-based view struggles to normalize those cases in which uses of public power properly understood as instances of political corruption seem nevertheless to have positive distributive externalities. Our separation of the descriptive characterization of uses of powers of office as "corrupt" from the evaluation of their wrongness and the graduation of normative judgments along the two dimensions of end-state and interactive justice provide our account with the antibodies against these problems. It can thus enhance both the descriptive and the normative analyses of this phenomenon.

A final contrast we would like to draw is more specific to the discussion in democratic theory and is centered on Mark Warren's idea that political corruption is wrong because it is a form of "duplicitous exclusion," which undermines the principle of democratic equality (Warren 2004, 2006). Relevant forms of political corruption concern the "contamination" of the democratic process with private—political, financial, and economic—interests. This contamination, which occurs, for example, in the case of private electoral campaign financing, is problematic insofar as it entails a distortion of the mechanisms of democratic representation

---

[32] In Rothstein and Varraich's words, "[to] say that something or someone is corrupt is doubtless a normative judgement" (2017, 131). Similarly, Miller has bluntly written that "corrupt actions are immoral actions" (2017, 2). The need to distinguish the descriptive analysis of corruption from its normative assessment is also recognized in Lessig (2018, 33).

(Warren 2004, 337). This distortion is wrong because it is a form of exclusion that violates the fundamental democratic principle of equal political inclusion: "Every individual potentially affected by a collective decision should have an opportunity to affect the decision proportional to his or her stake in the outcome" (Warren 2004, 337). The establishment of corrupt mechanisms of representation violates this principle, for it allows certain (classes of) citizens to buy a greater political influence for themselves to the detriment of those who do not partake in these mechanisms.

Unlike what we saw with impartiality-based accounts, Warren readily admits that not all breaches of the principle of democratic inclusion are wrong because they are corrupt. A distinctive feature of the exclusion that political corruption generates is a degree of hypocrisy on the part of corrupt agents, who are—Warren is adamant—always ready to "pay lip service" to the norms of democracy while they distort them by their conduct (Warren 2004, 333; 2006, 804). Because corrupt exclusion is thus "duplicitous," it is a feature of covert actions; if corrupt actions were to be taken in the open, their inherent hypocrisy would be revealed in a way that is not sustainable for the corrupt agents.

Qualifying the breaches of the democratic equality principle that are wrong because they are corrupt shields this view from the accusation of overreaching, which—as seen—affects the impartiality-based approaches. However, while this normative account of political corruption pinpoints an important form that this phenomenon may take in a democracy, we also think it is not completely satisfactory because it is too narrowly focused. There are good reasons to adopt our broader normative view grounded in office accountability. Let us see why.

A first obvious sense in which the democratic-equality-based normative view of political corruption is too narrowly focused is that, quite plainly, it makes sense of the wrongness of this phenomenon only within a democratic institutional setting. In contrast, our office-accountability-based view is relevant for various kinds of systems of rule-governed roles whereby entrusted powers are exercised. This broader institutional setup seems desirable in view of the many faces of political corruption and the empirical observation that it is a pathology not limited to democratic functions.

A second, perhaps less obvious consideration concerns the exclusive attention that the democratic-equality-based view dedicates to corrupt political action as covert action. As seen, Warren is persuaded that corrupt political agents are distinctively hypocritical because they declare themselves faithful to the democratic norm of egalitarian representation (e.g., they stand by the electoral mechanism when they run for office) but violate it by their actions (e.g., by becoming entangled in clientele or patronage practices). The corrupt agent's conduct as a means of excluding those who have rightful claims to democratic inclusion is thus concealed from public scrutiny. It is empirically accurate to notice that in many of its instances political corruption consists in secretive action. However, this concealment is not definitive of the practice either logically or empirically. To understand this point, it is sufficient to rethink both the practice of private financing of electoral campaigns in such countries as the United States (where the practice is legal, well regulated, and, thus, carried out in the open) and shamelessly paraded instances of systemic political corruption of which everyone is aware (e.g., systems of patronage in developing democracies). The democratic-equality-based view of political corruption sits uncomfortably with the normative analysis of any such nonsecretive instance. As argued in Chapter 1, our office-accountability-based view is capable of making sense of both the "hypocrisy" of corrupt agents and the lack of concealment of many of their actions. In our view, the marker of an officeholder's corrupt action is not that it is being concealed but that it is being animated by an agenda whose rationale *may not* be vindicated as coherent with the terms of the officeholder's power mandate. Because corrupt actions are so animated, corrupt agents tend to redescribe the logic of the agenda they pursue to make it resonate with the terms of their mandate (e.g., bribes are presented as tokens of appreciation). In this sense, their agenda is not necessarily (although it can be) a hidden agenda (see Ceva and Ferretti 2018, 221). It might be common knowledge that one politician entertains relations of clientele with her voters; these relations may even be lawful (as is often the case with private electoral campaign financing). Nevertheless, such relations are wrong because they respond to a patron–client logic that is extraneous to that of democratic representation that should govern the politician's action in coherence with her power mandate. As extensively argued in this chapter, this feature makes such actions interactively unjust even in the absence of the duplicitous nature that Warren ascribes to them.

In closing, note that the account of political corruption centered on democratic equality is affected by the same problem of providing a normatively laden definition of political corruption that we raised with reference to the impartiality-based approach. The capacity of our argument to separate the descriptive from the normative analysis of political corruption allows refining the content and scope of the moral assessment of this phenomenon. This feature reinforces the condemnatory power of calling something "corrupt" by avoiding the inflationary tendency that risks stretching this category by rendering its use idle or uninformative.

6. Conclusion

In this chapter, we have shown how and why there are good reasons not to limit the normative assessment of political corruption to considerations of the wrongness of its (actual or foreseeable; endogenous or exogenous) consequences. We have argued for the importance of supplementing the consequentialist mainstream with a deontological assessment of the inherent wrongness of political corruption as a specific form of interactive injustice consisting in a violation of the duty of office accountability. This assessment allows us to see how political corruption can be structurally wrong for the unjust relations it constitutes between officeholders as they exercise their interrelated powers of office. Political corruption thus works as an internal enemy of public institutions and is, therefore, pro tanto wrong. Because interactive justice is one dimension of justice, we have also explained that the all-things-considered judgment of the wrongness of political corruption may be quite nuanced. So, it could be excused facing countervailing considerations of end-state justice, or even discounted when it occurs against the background of unjust or illegitimate public institutions. The assessment of political corruption should, in this sense, always consider the institutional circumstances in which the relevant uses of a power of office occur.

As we argue in the remainder of the book, understanding political corruption as a form of interactive injustice has weighty implications for the design of anticorruption strategies as well as for the state's responsibility to implement them through use of its coercive power. Interpreting the wrongness of political corruption as an interactive injustice entails that anticorruption measures be in place as a deontological tenet of a public ethics of office. These measures may not be left entirely to a cost-benefit analysis, depending on the costs of anticorruption and the potential economic and political benefits that certain episodes of political corruption may provide in certain contexts but should be opposed as inherently wrong. It is thus a basic claim of a public ethics of office that the state's institutions are legitimated and required to use their coercive power to implement measures to counter political corruption as a matter of interactive justice in order to remedy the violation of the duty of office accountability in which the wrongness of political corruption consists.

This last set of considerations is helpful in fleshing out the positive side of our argument too. Notably, our office-accountability-based argument is the bedrock for the positive characterization of a public ethics of office proper of an interactively just institutional system. We should cherish establishing an institutional system that realizes the accountability of its constitutive offices because it is appropriately responsive to the normative status of officeholders to whom a justification of the uses of powers of office is owed in virtue of the interrelatedness of their institutional roles.[33] This interrelatedness is the source of the duty of office accountability whose fulfillment ensures that officeholders receive and offer appropriate treatment in performing their institutional functions. As we have shown, political corruption necessarily frustrates this requirement, and, therefore, officeholders should react to it to realize interactive justice in their institutions. To appreciate this sense of the wrongness of political corruption as a problem of public ethics grounds the promotion of office accountability in public institutions by focusing on the practical guidance for officeholders' interrelated actions to ensure institutional well-functioning. The next step in our argument requires clarifying who bears the moral responsibility for taking action vis-à-vis political corruption in order to bring such structures into being.

[33] Feinberg (1970c) is one of the *loci classici* for a discussion of the inherent value of the relations of mutual accountability between rights-holders. See also Young (1990).

4

Responsibility
for political corruption

1. Introduction

In this chapter, we address the question of who is responsible for political corruption. We interpret this question as referring to a practice of "answerability" within the context of a public ethics of office accountability. The object of our analysis is the practice of calling officeholders to respond for the uses they make of the powers entrusted to their institutional role, when they act in their interrelated institutional capacity, by reference to the terms of their power mandates. So, if "office accountability" is a regulative principle of officeholders' institutional conduct, "answerability" refers to a set of concrete institutional communicative practices, such as question time or periodical auditing in which officeholders are called to respond for acting or failing to act on their duty of office (see Watson 2004, 273–75; Duff 2018, 189; Hart 1968).

The duty at the core of practices of institutional answerability derives from the primary duty of office accountability. As seen in Chapter 3, officeholders have a primary duty of office to use the powers entrusted to their institutional role for the pursuit of an agenda whose rationale may be vindicated as coherent with the terms of their power mandate. The negative side of this positive duty of office commands that officeholders stand clear of political corruption. The secondary duty of answerability requires that officeholders answer in good faith for their conduct by reckoning with the rationale of the agenda they pursue in their

Political Corruption. Emanuela Ceva and Maria Paola Ferretti, Oxford University Press (2021). © Oxford University Press. DOI: 10.1093/oso/9780197567869.003.0005

institutional capacity. When called to answer for political corruption, officeholders might simply admit their corrupt behavior or their participation in a corrupt institutional practice. But an officeholder's answer might also be exculpatory by showing that the conduct under scrutiny followed an agenda whose rationale was fully coherent with the terms of the relevant power mandate; otherwise, officeholders might claim an excuse. An officeholder is blameworthy when she fails to answer for her conduct by delivering an exculpatory or excusatory response based on the requirements of office accountability. In this way, we distinguish answerability from liability to blame or punishment, which may intervene only in cases when *retrospective* responsibility for political corruption is established.

Officeholders who are retrospectively blameworthy for political corruption acquire new *prospective* responsibilities (in addition to the responsibilities normally associated with their role) so as to ensure that their institution functions in keeping with its raison d'être. These prospective responsibilities (such as accepting punishment or apologizing) are assigned in response to an officeholder's violation of her primary duty of office accountability. However, we argue, in some cases officeholders must take up their prospective responsibility independently of the attribution of retrospective responsibilities to any one of them specifically. This is because officeholders, as an interrelated group of institutional role occupants, share the prospective responsibility to make their institution well-functioning. In this sense, we show how officeholders have the "interrelated responsibility" to respond to political corruption by taking institutional action to restore just institutional relations. This responsibility gives content to the officeholders' anticorruption obligations, as we discuss in the next chapter where we characterize anticorruption as an integral part of a public ethics of office accountability.

It bears pointing out that officeholders must answer to charges of political corruption concerning their corrupt individual conduct as well as their participation in corrupt institutional practices. This is because assigning responsibility for political corruption does not merely mean expressing a negative judgment of some officeholders' conduct (or their character); it means, most importantly, recalling them to their duty of office accountability in consideration of the structural relations that occur between them in their institutional capacity. In Chapter 2, we defended the idea that corrupt institutional practices can be explained as a failure of the officeholders' interrelated action to uphold the raison d'être of their institution. As we proceed, we argue that officeholders may be held responsible for a deficit of office accountability as concerns their individual conduct in their institutional capacity or their involvement in corrupt institutional practices. What exactly this responsibility amounts to and what its implications are from the perspective of a public ethics of office is our primary concern in the present chapter.

The practice of holding officeholders answerable consists in engaging them in communication and in inviting them to respond for their conduct by admitting or rebutting the claims questioning the rationale of their guiding agendas. It is also a practice in which officeholders, by questioning their own conduct, reflect on the terms of their mandate and the use of their power of office against the background of the raison d'être of their institution. We thus focus on an interpersonal practice that consists of the interaction between those who call for answerability and those who are held answerable; solicits the normative engagement of the parties involved; and reconsiders the relations among them. The point of this communicative practice is not just to clarify the wrongdoing of a particular officeholder or of a constellation of officeholders in the interrelatedness of their roles. The practice of answerability is aimed primarily at identifying conduct that is disruptive of just institutional relations. This task is important for an adequate understanding of officeholders' retrospective responsibilities for political corruption. It also has important implications for understanding, prospectively, how best to attend to the task of restoring the interactive justice disrupted by political corruption.

The characterization of political corruption as an interactive injustice points at the salience of officeholders taking up prospective responsibilities as a matter of public ethics. From this perspective, the focus is not primarily on individual responsibilities to *repair* the damages caused by their corrupt conduct, for example, by compensating people whom some corrupt practices may have materially penalized. Nor is it just a matter of expressing contempt for an officeholder's misgivings. The main question at hand is how a public institution, as a system of embodied interrelated roles, should react to unjust institutional relations and how these relations may be corrected by restoring their interactive justice. This aspiration can be realized, for example, by making public institutions more supportive of anticorruption. However diverse these measures may be, we shall argue, they all respond to the same logic of upholding the duty of office accountability in a framework of a public ethics of office.

We begin this chapter by discussing some difficulties in assigning retrospective (§2) and prospective (§3) responsibility understood in terms of the causal contribution to an end-state wrong as addressed in the work of some institutionalists. We identify the function of the practice of holding officeholders answerable for political corruption as that of maintaining or restoring just institutional relations. This understanding provides the basis for offering a complete explanation of what it means to hold officeholders—severally and as interrelated via institutional structures—responsible for political corruption, both retrospectively and prospectively (§4). We then analyze particular retrospective and prospective answers to different cases of officeholders' responsibility for political corruption as captured by the summative (§5), morphological (§6), and systemic (§7) models of political corruption in institutional practices. We briefly conclude (§8) with some remarks on the practice of officeholders' answerability for political corruption as an integral part of a public ethics of office accountability.

2. Retrospective responsibility for political corruption

When advocates of the thesis of discontinuity between individual and institutional corruption, such as Dennis Thompson, affirm the need to shift attention from individual behaviors and characters to institutional mechanisms and practices, one of their main concerns is the assignment of responsibility for corruption. Responsibility is *difficult to assign* when corruption in a public institution is pervasive, and relations of cause and effect between individual actions and institutional practices are blurred. Yet even when individual officeholders can be appropriately characterized as agents of corruption (which suggests some form of causal responsibility), the practice of finger-pointing does not seem very *fruitful* in terms of indicating ways out of the corrupt institutional practices (see Thompson 1980).

For example, during electoral campaigns in Russia, the imprisonment of some high-level officials for allegations of corruption has become a political ritual instrumental in reinvigorating popular consensus. In the 2018 electoral campaign, Abdusamad Gamidov, a top official in the southern autonomous republic of Dagestan, and two regional governors, Kirov's Nikita Belykh and Sakhalin's Alexander Khoroshavin, were given long-term prison sentences, which Vladimir Putin in his campaign emphasized as evidence of his commitment to opposing corruption. These officials had enjoyed years of governmental support, even though their corrupt activities were well known to the public and the government alike. Their conviction was certainly responsive to their wrongful conduct. However, there are good reasons to think that the impact of these events on reducing corruption in the country has been and will be negligible. Typically, after voting results are announced, no actual policies are, in fact, implemented to systematically tackle corrupt practices and, often, new corrupt governors replace the dismissed ones.

When political corruption is entrenched in institutional practices, even when blameworthy individual behavior is censored and perhaps responsible individuals are banned from public office, the practice may still endure. This claim is crucial to understand the institutionalists' argumentation. Institutionalists would not deny that in cases of individual corruption (and in some cases of institutional corruption too) responsibility is appropriately assigned retrospectively to individual officeholders. They object, however, to what they regard as the practice of shaming, blaming, and punishing individual officeholders because it cannot lead to appropriate and effective answers to the question of assigning prospective responsibilities for corruption and anticorruption.

In what follows, we discuss the institutionalists' claim that—retrospectively—identifying the causal and moral responsibility of individual officeholders in corrupt institutional practices is difficult and sometimes impossible. In §3, we turn to the institutionalists' objection that even when it is possible, the retrospective assignment of individual responsibilities for political corruption may be inappropriate for the sake of finding—prospectively—adequate answers to this phenomenon.

Establishing responsibility for political corruption is a moral exercise. In our view, responsibility is not just a matter of empirical causation; a normative source of responsibility is to be found in the rationale of the agenda pursued by an officeholder's contested conduct. According to a standard view, moral responsibility aptly attracts blameworthiness.[1] Holding an officeholder morally responsible presupposes that she has the capacity for practical

---

[1] For a discussion of whether there can be morally responsible behavior that is neither praiseworthy nor blameworthy, see, for example, Zimmerman (1988, 61–62).

reasoning, the moral/political understanding of her mandate, as well as a measure of freedom, in the sense that it would be possible for her to act otherwise. These conditions distinguish moral responsibility from pure causality. Causal responsibility, in the absence of understanding, free will, and intention, does not generally entail blameworthiness.[2] These conditions also presuppose that when agents act under coercion or duress, they may be morally excused or their moral responsibility can be mitigated.

A basic claim of some institutionalists is that when an officeholder operates within a systemically corrupt environment, to whose establishment she has not directly contributed, there may be elements that exclude or weaken her moral responsibility (Thompson 1980, 905–6). However, we think that even in these cases an argument can be made to show the extent to which individual officeholders retain moral responsibility for their conduct. In a corrupt environment, an officeholder may act in a corrupt manner because he gives in to peer pressure to adapt to an institutional practice. This adaptation is the result of some kind of instrumental reasoning that can be seen as a response to a desire to "fit in," or to avoid the personal or professional costs of noncompliance (e.g., mobbing, loss of privileges, and professional prestige). In these cases, we could say that officeholders retain moral responsibility for their individual conduct because, by deciding to adapt, they exercise their agency. In most of these cases, we cannot say that corrupt agents are coerced or manipulated (circumstances that presuppose the suppression of their agency). Corrupt officeholders can be held morally responsible because whenever they are faced with the choice between complying with a corrupt practice or resisting it and paying the corresponding price (e.g., undermining their career prospects), they engage in practical reasoning and make choices.

---

[2] The relationships between causal responsibility, moral responsibility, blameworthiness, and their relationships with restorative justice are the object of a wide debate. See, for example, Copp (1997); Sher (2006); Waller (2011); and Wolf (1990).

To the extent that officeholders retain their agency, their action can be morally assessed and they can be held blameworthy for it.[3]

While we cannot generally say that the agency of an officeholder who gives in to systemic corruption is suppressed, one could still argue that it is challenged and twisted. This observation points to the mitigating effects that involvement in a corrupt institutional practice may have for assigning individual retrospective responsibility. Surely, these effects may not relieve officeholders from their responsibility altogether, but they may make the assignment of moral responsibility less than straightforward. This is a special concern for institutionalists, who consider individual corrupt actions only in view of their contribution to some kind of end-state institutional wrong (e.g., the loss of institutional trustworthiness or the systematic violation of some citizens' rights), or when such individual actions are triggered by a corrupt motive or trait of character (see the discussion in Chapter 3, §2).

Institutionalists who accept that institutional corruption could not occur if there were no individual agents of corruption also think that it is appropriate to hold officeholders responsible for institutional corruption only proportionally to their direct or indirect causal contribution to establishing and maintaining a corrupt institutional practice (in terms of both their actions and omissions).[4] From their point of view, it seems that we have good reason to discount, at least in part, the individual responsibility of officeholders who work for a corrupt institution. This is because their moral responsibility is weakened proportionally to the freedom they have had to distance their actions from the net of behavior leading to corruption. So, for example, some institutionalists would point out that, within a system where the work of lobbies is normalized, to

---

[3] For an extensive discussion through the lens of the model of "coercion by threat," see Bagnoli (2018) and Bagnoli and Ceva (mimeo).

[4] Thompson (2005, 16) complains that "the charges are brought against the few 'bad apples' who misbehaved, even if the conduct in less egregious form is widespread and cultivated by the institution."

put the blame for institutional corruption on an officeholder who gives in to a lobbyist's pressures when setting the priorities of her political agenda would mean not to take seriously the power that lobbies have come to exercise. In this institutionalist view, the main cause of corruption is not the politician's conduct but the institutional mechanism that sanctions the lobby's disproportionate power in setting political priorities.

These concerns are warranted when trying to establish an officeholder's individual *causal* retrospective responsibility within a corrupt institutional practice. In the first place, an officeholder's participation in a corrupt institutional practice may not reflect or be explained by reference to the officeholder's personal motives or a vice of her character. But the concerns run even deeper and regard the structural interactions between the participants in a corrupt institutional practice. Recall the example concerning the procedures of the call for tenders we discussed in Chapter 2 as an instance of systemic corruption. It is indeed difficult to establish the exact responsibility of any single contract official in a tender procedure, when the actual corrupt exchanges (e.g., the bribes) occur between construction companies and on-site engineers. In the context of systemic corruption, rules are often subverted long before corruption is denounced. It may be that officeholders realize that they are working in a corrupt manner without, however, being able to identify the individuals who have actually started to act corruptly and those who, instead, have only participated in the corrupt practice because of the interrelatedness of their institutional roles.

We concur that it is difficult to establish retrospectively *individual causal* responsibilities for political corruption when the corruption of a particular institutional practice is the result of the interrelated conduct of a multiplicity of agents. This difficulty is heightened when causal responsibility is meant to track an individual's contribution to establishing a wrongful institutional practice, which instantiates a form of end-state injustice (consisting, e.g., in the violation of someone's subjective rights or opportunities). This complication occurs because, in these circumstances, the corruption of a practice is actually the product of a complex web of repeated interactions of multiple agents at different points in time whose individual roles are hard to identify and assess. The complexity of this structure of interaction creates obvious difficulties in assigning responsibility for corruption to the extent that responsibility is understood as the *causation* or the *contribution* of an individual agent to a certain institutional outcome.

This causal or contributive understanding of responsibility creates problems for those who defend a reductionist view, according to which those who cause institutional corruption are responsible for it. This is, for instance, Seumas Miller's position (Miller 2017, 134). Because corrupt institutional practices are often complex, the dimensions of the contributions to their establishment and maintenance on the part of any one agent are often incommensurable or difficult to assess. Thompson (1980) has presented this complexity as a variation of the so-called problem of "the many hands," in which a certain result is due to the action of many agents, but it is not easy to disentangle the individual contributions to that result and evaluate them from a moral point of view.

Miller (2017, 134) suggests that in order to address the problem of who is responsible for a corrupt institutional practice, we should focus on the "collective responsibility for *joint actions* of human beings in their capacity as institutional role occupants" (emphasis added). Miller explains this suggestion as follows: For any given institution, there is an institutional joint obligation to serve a certain end, and each individual officeholder is expected to perform certain actions in order to pursue that end. In other words, all officeholders have the obligation to serve the designated institutional purpose. The relevant questions in cases of political corruption concern the *ways* in which officeholders, as a group, can fail to discharge such an obligation, who should be held responsible for that *failure*, and whether officeholders can—as a group—be held *jointly* responsible for it.

Can we say that even when it is just one officeholder who fails to perform the actions required by her role, the whole group fails to fulfill its institutional obligation? Miller (2017, 136–37) seems to suggest that we cannot; in fact, he explains that in most cases, officeholders should be held morally responsible only for their *actual* contribution to the corrupt institutional practice. Because, for Miller, causal responsibility can generate moral responsibility only when it entails some degree of intentionality—or at least it excludes ignorance or action under compulsion—it seems particularly hard to establish when an institutional practice becomes the responsibility of each and every officeholder in the institution. Miller (2017, 136–37) himself points out that joint moral responsibility is appropriately assigned to officeholders when the following threefold condition obtains: Each and every officeholder (1) has causally contributed to the pursuit of the institutional end; (2) has had the intention of pursuing that end; and (3) has prioritized that end in her action. When this threefold condition obtains, it is easy to see how officeholders are jointly responsible for discharging their institutional obligation. However, the failure to discharge that obligation is harder to explain in terms of joint responsibility because in cases of institutional corruption the agents' individual causal responsibilities are typically very diverse, in terms of motivation, priorities, and actual contribution.

The examples discussed in Chapter 2 show how Miller's account of joint responsibility does not capture most cases of corrupt institutional practices. The case of the Willy Brandt Berlin Airport illustrates how diverse the interests and priority ranks are among the many actors involved in the corrupt institutional practice of assigning a tender on the basis of a "low bid," with the tacit understanding that price increases would be subsequently approved. Imtech management's urgent need to save the finances of their constructing company, as well as the local politicians' need to be faithful to their electoral promises, guided the various agents' actions in upholding the "low-bid" practice without explicit concertation. Moreover, none of them can be said to have acted with the shared intent of causing the failure of the airport project, nor—in most cases—can we say that they have causally and willfully contributed to the delays and additional costs incurred during the works. Indeed, in this case, as in many cases of corrupt institutional practices, only some officeholders can be said to have explicitly failed to act in accordance with the institutional requirements of their roles. What we can regularly see is a variety of motivations and finalities, so that typically officeholders act without the implicit goal of making the institution deviate from its purpose. That being the case, our discussion shows how causal-reductionist approaches to joint action such as Miller's do not fare well in terms of establishing moral responsibilities for corrupt institutional practices.

Contrary to this teleological logic, our deontological account of the wrongness of political corruption can help to assign officeholders moral responsibility for political corruption. Our interactive-justice-based account can hold officeholders answerable for the rationale that guides their exercise of their powers of office, both severally as individual institutional role occupants and considered in their interrelatedness. Appreciating this shift requires and entails a change of perspective from the end-state injustices produced through a corrupt institutional practice to the interactive injustice inherent to the practice itself. In our view, the assignment of retrospective moral responsibility for political corruption concerns primarily the deficit of office accountability as regards the rationale of the agenda pursued by the officeholders' individual or interrelated conduct (as we argue more extensively in §4). This deficit of office accountability may be either a matter of discrete (in the case of an officeholder's individual corrupt conduct) or interrelated (in the case of a corrupt institutional practice) action (or omission). Reconsider, from our perspective, the case of the Berlin Brandenburg Willy Brandt Airport, in which we cannot disentangle the contributions of single officeholders to the corruption of a certain institutional practice. Now, even in such cases, it is sufficient to indicate that officeholders participated in a practice that fails to uphold office accountability. This failure is inherently wrong as a form of interactive injustice because it instantiates an alteration of the normative order of interactions that officeholders entertain in their institutional capacity. This injustice is the wrong for which corrupt officeholders are morally responsible. Therefore, holding them blameworthy for that injustice tracks their wrongdoing and falls in the appropriate remit of retrospective responsibility.

Importantly, this discussion helps dispel the doubt that by assigning to officeholders retrospective responsibility for a corrupt institutional practice independently of their actual contribution to that practice, we apply charges of political corruption indistinctively. Returning to the practices of favoritism illustrated in Chapter 2, suppose that a new member joins the faculty of an academic school just before a new position is advertised. The newly appointed professor is not part of the hiring committee for the new position. The hiring committee makes a job offer to a candidate who had previously worked in a research team supervised by a committee member. The offer follows a logic of favoritism that was established and normalized in the department during previous years. Suppose now that some of the excluded candidates address a complaint to the head of the school by flagging a possible conflict of interest. During the internal investigation, the new professor is questioned about the department's recruitment procedures and whether he is aware of patterns of favoritism. Could he refuse any implication by pointing out that he has just joined the department and was not directly involved in the procedure under scrutiny? Could he simply suggest that only the members of the committee should be answerable for favoritism? Or is there reason to think that he should claim responsibility for what happens in his department? This is a worrisome doubt especially because the last question may lead to the concern that we fail to take seriously the differences among individuals and avoid tracking actual wrongdoing by individual officeholders. But in this section, we have shown how officeholders can be assigned *moral* responsibility for the interactive injustice of political corruption independently of establishing their *causal* responsibility in bringing about some form of end-state wrong (e.g., the loss of institutional trustworthiness, or the penalization of some candidates for a job). Thus, the new professor in our example assumes moral responsibility for the interactive injustice instantiated in the practice of favoritism that has developed in his department even if he did not contribute to establishing it. As we will see in the remainder of this chapter, by his action, the professor's duty of office accountability requires him to sustain the well-functioning of the department also by calling his new colleagues to answer for their conduct. By denying any involvement in the hiring process, he evades this type of commitment and is thereby exposed to moral blame for altering the normative order of interactions within the department. Thus, our deontological approach to the wrongness of political corruption has the resources to assign officeholders retrospective responsibilities for establishing a corrupt institutional practice and in this way attending to the institutionalists' first objection regarding the difficulty of this task.

3. Prospective responsibility for political corruption

To fully appreciate the significance of the change of perspective that we suggest, we must clarify the point of assigning moral responsibility for political corruption. As John Stuart Mill (1963–91, 458–60) remarked, even if the concept of moral responsibility stands in a complex relation with that of free will—and there are a number of metaphysical quarrels about that relation—there is a basic sense in which the very reason to ask whether someone is justifiably considered morally responsible for her wrongdoing is that we want to know what could make things better. For example, we are interested in moral responsibility because we want to establish whether punishment can be the satisfactory answer to someone's wrongful conduct, which means that, say, we want to know whether we can thus influence the wrongdoer's behavior so as to avoid future wrongs.

When we assess moral responsibilities for political corruption, we suggest that the point of holding officeholders responsible is to understand how we can signal that a certain kind of conduct is corrupt and wrong as such, end that corrupt conduct, promote institutional practices of office accountability, and restore just institutional relations in the future. In an important sense, even punishment in the anticorruption discourse seldom has a prominent reparative function. Often it is simply the answer that is due to a particular wrongdoing, in the sense of openly condemning a certain conduct, or rather it is thought of as a deterrent to future corruption, for example, in the form of monetary disincentives.

In this regard, we agree with Thompson (1980, 907) and Lessig (2013, 17), who criticize legalistic approaches to corruption and anticorruption, which are mainly focused on singling out, removing from office, and punishing corrupt individuals. For institutionalists, we should try to establish individual retrospective responsibilities whenever possible; but they are also very critical of finger-pointing within a corrupt institutional setting. From this point of view, institutionalists stress that it has been a major flaw of contemporary attempts to oppose political corruption to concentrate mainly on major scandals of individual corruption (e.g., bribery), thereby losing sight of the systemic features of corruption and the steps necessary to remedy it, besides punishing blameworthy individuals (Miller et al. 2005, 8–9). This plea reflects the institutionalists' concerns about assigning responsibility for corruption to individual politicians who give in to the pressure from lobbies within a system that sanctions the lobbies' function and affirms their power.

We share Thompson's and Lessig's preoccupation with an entirely reparative understanding of the practice of holding individual officeholders answerable for corrupt institutional practices. Nevertheless, we argue that there is some important room for assigning responsibilities for political corruption to officeholders, both severally and as interrelated via institutional structures. To do so, we should consider the way in which practices of answerability may serve to establish several kinds of retrospective responsibilities, which may prompt a plurality of reactions at the institutional level. For individual wrongdoers, the assignment of retrospective responsibilities not only publicly states the wrongness of that conduct, but also gives rise to a new set of prospective responsibilities—for example, to apologize, repair, or restore. In these cases, the acceptance of someone's prospective individual responsibilities, such as that to accept punishment or to apologize, is the appropriate answer to a violation of office accountability. However, and more generally, to the extent that the point of holding officeholders responsible for political corruption is to restore relations of office accountability, the primary function of the practice of answerability is not to be maximally censorious or to punish blameworthy individuals. The point of this practice should not be reduced to reparation for end-state injustices caused by a corrupt conduct (e.g., its material damages). The practice of answerability should primarily pinpoint and address the interactive injustice instantiated in political corruption in order to restore just institutional relations between officeholders in the exercise of their institutional functions.[5] The practice of answerability thus involves questioning who is allegedly retrospectively responsible for what has gone wrong and soliciting a reaction from them. This is a way to bring the alleged wrongdoer to acknowledge the moral and political significance of his corrupt conduct.[6] Practices of answerability have the potential to activate a normative change in the person

---

[5] For the emphasis on the relational dimension of restorative justice in contrast with reparative approaches, see Duff (2017).
[6] On the communicative aspects of blame, see, for example, Fricker (2016).

to whom retrospective responsibility is assigned. In this sense, practices of answerability are a matter of assigning *moral* responsibility (not just establishing *causal* responsibility).

A key aspect of discussing political corruption within a public ethics of office is to appreciate that officeholders held answerable for political corruption are not simply exposed to a judgment of blameworthiness in the occurrence of an interactive injustice. They are most importantly engaged in a communicative justificatory practice and thus have the opportunity to rebut the charges of failing to comply with the duty of office accountability binding on their role. That is, the officeholders who answer for their conduct may reject retrospective responsibility for political corruption by showing how the rationale of their agenda may in fact withstand the scrutiny of office accountability; or else, they could adduce excusatory elements—for example, by pointing at the effects of their action under nonideal circumstances in terms of enhancing end-state justice.[7] In the former case, officeholders would deflect retrospective responsibility for the interactive wrongs of political corruption; in the latter, they would claim that their retrospective responsibility should be mitigated. In other cases, officeholders may answer by acknowledging the wrongness of certain behaviors or practices and, thus, admitting their retrospective responsibility.

To hold officeholders responsible for political corruption aims at a normative change in the officeholders' conduct. This change is pursued by fostering an increased normative alignment in interpreting how officeholders should discharge their power mandate between those who hold answerable and those who are held answerable for their uses of a power of office.[8] This change may occur, for example, by bringing to bear appropriate reasons or

---

[7] For the trade-offs between the interactive and the end-state dimensions of justice, see Chapter 3, §4.

[8] Moral alignment is discussed in Williams (1995) and Fricker (2016). For a discussion of the misalignment of reasons in cases of individual involvement in systemic corruption, see Ceva and Radoilska (2018).

contextual considerations that were originally sidelined. For example, accused of giving in to the demands of certain lobbies, an officeholder may initiate a discussion with her colleagues about the legitimate role of lobbies in politics and what may be required of individual officeholders in terms of resisting pressure from corporate interests. An officeholder may even admit her wrongdoing. At the same time, she may expose the difficulties encountered in the face of pressures from lobbyists. By becoming aware of these difficulties and engaging critically on the legitimate terms of their dealings with lobbyists in their institutional capacity, officeholders may decide to introduce more effective support and supervision measures to prevent political corruption from recurring. More generally, the practice of holding officeholders answerable for political corruption is necessary to promote a normative alignment among the occupants of interrelated institutional roles and, thus, to enable the practical change required to overcome political corruption and possibly to prevent it from occurring anew. The communicative nature and the mutuality of this practice are internally consistent with the logic of office accountability that should regulate the institutional interactions between officeholders.

From this point of view, we can appreciate an important relational feature of the practice of answerability within a public ethics of office accountability. This feature emerges by noticing that to assign retrospective responsibility for political corruption involves pondering the rationale of an officeholder's action according to criteria of office accountability; but it also significantly involves reconsidering the patterns of interrelatedness of institutional roles, the division of tasks among the role occupants, and the definition of the terms of the power mandate by which different roles are entrusted. Tackling these elements is crucial to restore the normative order of interactions that political corruption disrupts.

In sum, we have pinpointed so far that to hold officeholders answerable for their conduct in their institutional capacity means two things. First, it is a way to assign retrospective responsibility, which involves a moral judgment that points at an officeholder's failure to attend to her duty of office accountability (hence the assignment of blameworthiness). Second, and even more importantly we believe, practices of answerability have—prospectively—the purpose of engaging the officeholder normatively. Answerability practices open the opportunity for a change as concerns both an officeholder's individual conduct and some institutional practices that occur in virtue of the interrelation between the officeholder's conduct and the conduct of the other officeholders who act in their institutional capacity.

In a prospective sense, assigning moral responsibility is a way to ask for things to be otherwise in the future. The reason why we look retrospectively at responsibility is, as seen, because we want to gain a better understanding of what has gone wrong (e.g., which officeholders violated office accountability and whether certain institutional dynamics have favored that corrupt conduct), and we also want to be better equipped prospectively to enable officeholders to stand clear of political corruption. This prospective focus holds not only for individuals, but also for corrupt public institutions, with a view to upholding just institutional relations. This is the extent of our agreement with Thompson's and Lessig's qualm, according to which even if we could overcome the difficulties of assigning individual responsibilities within corrupt institutions, the predominant practice of individualized finger-pointing and the related blaming and shaming of single officeholders *in isolation* cannot, by itself, be an adequate response to corrupt institutional practices. However, it should be clear by now that looking at corrupt institutional practices from an individualized perspective is not an oxymoron. In particular, the practice of holding individual officeholders answerable for their corrupt conduct does not necessarily entail overlooking the systemic features of corrupt institutional practices. To the contrary, we have shown how answerability practices are most appropriately conceived as embedded in public institutions. In the next section, we fill in the details of such practices by further fleshing out their retrospective and prospective components.

4. Responsibility for corrupt institutional practices

We have already mentioned that any officeholder can be held answerable for a corrupt institutional practice, irrespectively of the particular causal or contributive retrospective responsibility she has had in establishing that practice. Reconstructing causal links and individual contributions to political corruption may be part of the story of what has gone wrong with a certain institutional practice. However, we have submitted that to assign responsibilities for political corruption to officeholders, both severally as individuals and interrelatedly as an institution, does not necessarily require disentangling and weighing each agent's single causal role or contribution to establishing a corrupt practice. A promising way forward consists in pointing at the interrelatedness of institutional roles and the ways in which the exercises of power associated with those roles may come to form a constellation (the corrupt institutional practice) that instantiates an interactive injustice.[9] Calling officeholders to answer for corrupt institutional practices has, in some cases, the function of making political corruption a matter for all institutional role occupants by recognizing patterns of interrelatedness between their roles and the exercises of power that come with them. Thus, retrospectively, we can assign responsibility for political corruption to officeholders as the interrelated members of an institution, even when not all of them are recognizably blameworthy as individuals, for example, because some of them were partly or fully unaware of the ongoing corrupt practice.

---

[9] See Chapter 3 and, for an earlier formulation, see Ceva (2019) and Ferretti (2019).

The pivot of our argument, as introduced in Chapter 2, is the view that political corruption is the attribute of an institutional practice in virtue of the interrelated conduct of the officeholders giving body to institutional roles. From this institutional perspective, the accountability of an officeholder's conduct does not concern first and foremost her action taken in isolation from that of the other role occupants within her institution. Rather, it must consider the officeholder's conduct in light of the structural interrelatedness of the various institutional roles. In this specific sense, we understand the officeholders' responsibility for corrupt institutional practices as "interrelated responsibility." Interrelated responsibility for political corruption is assigned to officeholders when the rationale of the agenda underpinning the uses of powers of office within an institutional practice may not be vindicated as coherent with the terms of their power mandates. Recall that the capacity of a public institution to operate in keeping with its raison d'être depends on each and every officeholder's accountable use of her powers of office. Therefore, it may be enough that just one or a (relatively) limited number of officeholders act corruptly to make other officeholders deviate (more or less advertently) from their mandate and to make a certain institutional practice go off track.

In Chapter 2, we described the different dynamics in light of which corrupt institutional practices may be understood as a function of the officeholders' interrelated conducts (we revisit those dynamics later). We should emphasize now that, in view of the thesis of continuity between officeholders' individual corrupt conduct and corrupt institutional practices, our understanding of political corruption reconciles individualism and collectivism, and it takes seriously both the distinction between persons and the interrelatedness of their institutional roles. That is, recognition of the continuity between the quality of officeholders' individual conduct and that of institutional practices suggests that there is a way of conceiving the corruption of an institution as an interrelated failure to keep the institution faithful to its raison d'être. Even if individual actions are explanatorily basic, the corruption of institutional practices can hardly be explained exhaustively by reference to the different officeholders' actions taken in isolation.[10] It is their structural interrelatedness that makes the officeholders' conducts relevant. So, we can talk of the officeholders as if they were a collective, but without assuming any kind of collective agency.[11] It is the interrelated exercise of their individual agency—when they act in their institutional capacity—that may constitute the interactive injustice in which the wrongness of political corruption consists. This interactive focus brings to the fore the assessment of the patterns of interaction through which certain powers of office are exercised, the officeholders' underpinning agenda, and the agenda's rationale, which must respond, as we have seen, to the logic of office accountability.

Consider one simplified scenario of interrelated responsibility first. A group of friends smash a window while playing football together in a yard. The window owner comes to the yard and asks who is to blame. Of course, the one who kicked the ball into the window was one particular player, but the friends now reflect on the fact that smashing the window was a result of their playing together. They realize that they had set the goal too close to the window and that the keeper performed poorly. So they conclude that it is more appropriate to recognize their retrospective responsibility, say that "they" smashed the window and "they" are to blame, and, thus, accept that "they" are required to take up the prospective responsibility, say, to pay for a new window.

---

[10] This interpretation resonates with Larry May's explanation of what a collective action is by pointing at the interrelation between the members of a group, rather than viewing it as a manifestation of transindividuality (see May 1977, 55).

[11] Our approach to group agency differs from a number of accounts that presuppose a collectivist methodology, including those based on linguistic analysis (French 1998, 37); shared intentions (Bratman 2013); and plural subject accounts (Gilbert 2000). Instead, there is a family resemblance between our interrelatedness approach and Larry May's (1992) concept of interdependence. According to May, interdependence is the basis for an account of collective responsibility that not only combines individualism and collectivism, but focuses on both relationships and social structures.

We suggest that taking up interrelated responsibility in the case of corrupt institutional practices follows the same logic: It is a way to articulate the observation that the misdoing consists in the interrelated conduct of various individuals who act in virtue of the powers entrusted to the roles they occupy within an institution. Our argument is that, facing a suspected deficit of office accountability in an institutional practice, we can call all officeholders in that institution interrelatedly to answer for the allegation of political corruption. The officeholders' acknowledgment of their interrelated responsibility has the function of shedding light on the kind of wrong that is taking place within a public institution. This retrospective understanding can also be instrumental in calling on the interrelated members of the institution to take up the *prospective* responsibility to react to that wrong. [12]

For example, a contract officer who is called on to give an account of the suspicious result of a tender procedure may answer for her decision by saying that she has actually assigned the contract to the bidder that had made the best offer in terms of price for quality. Nevertheless, it may be the case that this decision was not taken against a background of fair market competition—because (as in the case of the Willy Brandt Airport) it was, in fact, responsive to a corrupt practice of "low bid" subject to subsequent price increases. Even if some single officeholders have participated in the practice without deliberately intending to deviate from their power mandate, we can still say that, in virtue of the interrelatedness of their institutional roles, officeholders are implicated in and responsible for the corruption of the tendering process. In this specific sense, the officeholders' interrelated conduct (and its internal division of

---

[12] In this sense, we side with those authors who think that the question is not only about whether collective agents are morally responsible for wrongdoing, but about the reasons why we should hold them morally responsible. In some cases, attributions of responsibility are a way to acknowledge some pathologies of group dynamics or to facilitate the socialization of group members to act more responsibly in the future (List and Pettit 2011, 185).

roles) may have been such that they, as interrelated agents, have failed the raison dʼêtre of the institution. For example, the interplay of the efficiency reasons guiding some officeholders' actions, combined with the reasons of other officeholders moved by the prospect of a personal gain, may fail to ensure fair and impartial competition among potential contractors. Fairness in competition is arguably included in the raison dʼêtre of the institutional practice of a call for tenders and, therefore, the ground on which the mandates of the various powers of office were entrusted to the officeholders implicated in the procedure.

Asking what kind of incentives have guided the different participants in the corrupt practice, we may find a variety of motives and rationales. In some cases, the agenda guiding some officeholders' conduct may have had a rationale that is not obviously incoherent with their power mandate—for example, when one fails to report a rigged tender procedure in order not to stop some urgent construction works (e.g., of a new hospital ward to deal with a medical emergency). However, the officeholders, as an interrelated group, can be held morally responsible for the corrupt institutional procedure in the same way as the football mates are responsible for smashing the window as a group. A similar case concerns the charge of fraud that affected the Lombardy regional purchasing center in Italy during the COVID-19 outbreak. The investigation concerns the supply of half a million euros of hospital coats and other hospital equipment by the company Dama spa, managed by the brother-in-law of the governor of Lombardy, Attilio Fontana, and under 10% ownership by his wife.[13] Many individuals are investigated for their personal responsibility in the matter (e.g., who paid who), but our argument shows an important sense in which the judgment of corruption can be attributed to the institution of the regional purchasing center as constituted by a

---

[13] See https://www.ilsole24ore.com/art/lombardia-fontana-indagato-nell-inchiesta-fornitura-camici-ADutGKg?refresh_ce=1.

group of agents whose interrelated action reveals a deficit of office accountability.

As illustrated at many stages throughout this book, the wrong of political corruption may not be limited to the specific actions of specific agents (and their possible consequences). What is more, the wrong of partaking in a corrupt institutional practice is not reducible to a question of complicity in cases of political corruption in the sense that it is enough, for example, to be aware of the corrupt conduct of other officeholders to be involved in their wrongdoing.[14] Rather, the wrongness of corrupt institutional practices concerns—also and most significantly—the quality of the patterns of role-based interaction between its members. As seen, to make a judgment of political corruption means asking whether the rationale of the agenda informing an officeholder's conduct in her institutional capacity or an institutional practice can pass the test of office accountability. We have also seen how retrospectively it may not always be possible to establish and assess the different causal contributions of individual participants in a corrupt institutional practice (as the institutionalists lamented). What we can further appreciate now is how it is possible to identify and assess an institutional deficit of office accountability whenever certain institutional practices fail to operate in keeping with the raison d'être of the institution. Identifying this deficit has the heuristic function of revealing that something has gone wrong in the way officeholders work in their interrelation. This can be due to a variety of factors, including the officeholders' motives but also the particular division of roles or structural risk linked to the institutional functions. In this spirit, to hold officeholders responsible for political corruption can be a way to reassess the work of officeholders within a public institution and its coherence with the raison d'être of that institution.

---

[14] For some discussions of the notion of moral complicity, see, for example, Mellema (2016).

For the agents involved in a corrupt institutional practice to recognize their interrelated responsibility for political corruption means to acknowledge the importance of attending, as interrelated individuals, to deficits of office accountability within their institution. Taking up responsibility means, in an important sense, being ready to accept the prospective responsibility for restoring office accountability in institutional practices. Revisit, from this vantage point, the aforementioned example of a newly appointed member of the faculty in an academic school where practices of favoritism have become the norm. This new officeholder may be answerable for taking (or for failing to take) restorative actions (e.g., by reporting the corrupt practice to the university ethics committee) even in the total absence of retrospective responsibility on his part. This consideration indicates that the officeholders' acceptance of their interrelated responsibility for political corruption—rather than assigning individual retrospective responsibility to any one of them—is the crucial nexus between political corruption and the duty to restore just institutional relations. This is the crux for understanding officeholders' anticorruption obligations, as we discuss in Chapter 5.

Assigning interrelated responsibility for political corruption (both retrospectively and prospectively) to officeholders in their institutional capacity is not inconsistent with providing differentiated answers concerning the punishment of their individual acts, the redistribution of tasks among them, or the various ways in which they can be called to action. Indeed, while we can call an institutional practice "corrupt," only individual officeholders in that practice have the moral standing to be blameworthy, be punished, or take action to restore just institutional relations. Therefore, even if we can predicate the political corruption of institutional practices, the question of assigning particular prospective responsibilities to the officeholders involved in those practices is inescapable. We have already suggested that the logic of restoring just institutional relations requires that some prospective responsibilities (such as apologizing) be directly assigned to the officeholders who committed the relevant wrongdoing. We have also seen that other responsibilities may be assigned to or taken up by officeholders independently of their retrospective responsibilities, in virtue of their being in a privileged position to promote a positive change (e.g., because they occupy positions of leadership or they have access to information unavailable to others).

Because, as argued in Chapter 2, patterns of interrelatedness that instantiate corrupt institutional practices are different, the three models of political corruption in institutional practices that we have identified (summative, morphological, and systemic) point to different ways of disentangling and assigning responsibility for political corruption in different circumstances. The time has now come to illustrate such differences in detail. This illustration is not only a worthwhile clarification exercise of philosophical analysis. Against a "one-size-fits-all approach," we propose to look at different instances of political corruption using these models, so as to highlight different reasons for valuing the practice of assigning interrelated retrospective and prospective responsibilities for political corruption and identifying appropriate individual and institutional answers to it.

5. Responsibility for summative political corruption

When political corruption in institutional practices is of the summative kind, there is an obvious sense in which we can say that individual officeholders may have contributed to the corrupt practice, perhaps only as bystanders failing to denounce the practice or to try to stop it. Officeholders can thus be said to be severally retrospectively responsible for their individual conduct within the practice. Are they also morally responsible for the corrupt practice itself?

Recall from Chapter 2 the example of the customs officers' allowing the establishment of a money-smuggling practice within a border-control agency. In many cases of this kind, officeholders come short of their individual duties to prevent money smuggling and thus contribute to the failure of making the border agency well-functioning. To the extent that an officeholder has contributed to the corrupt practice (either by action or by omission and even absent an explicit concertation with other officeholders), there is a straightforward sense in which she can be said to be retrospectively responsible for the corruption of that practice and the wrongs thereby generated. Specifically, corrupt officeholders can be held individually responsible for their own contribution to the occurrence of an end-state injustice (e.g., the distributive injustice that money smuggling allows). However, on this count, officeholders could also reject full moral responsibility for the corrupt practice on the ground that their actual contribution to establishing that practice was very small (e.g., they can claim that they have acted only once and for a negligible sum of money). Alternatively, we could resort to Miller's category of joint action (see §2) and conclude that all officeholders can be held morally responsible as a group for allowing the institution to deviate from its purposes. However, as explained earlier, we could say so only if it is actually the case that each and every officeholder shares the same conduct (allowing smuggling) and purpose (private economic gain) with the others. But this condition seems particularly difficult to verify especially when the corrupt practice occurs at major border crossings and thus typically implicates several custom officers, teams of guards, and possibly seaport employees.

If we look at this case from our interactive-injustice-based perspective, we can see a promising way around these complications. When officeholders fail to behave following an agenda whose rationale may be vindicated as coherent with the terms of their power mandate (either by action or inaction), we can hold them individually morally responsible for violating their duty of office accountability, independently of the actual or expected consequences of their conduct. Moreover, because their interrelated action has summatively constituted a corrupt institutional practice, they can also be held interrelatedly retrospectively responsible for that practice and for the interactive injustice that has thus occurred.

Emphasizing the interactive injustice of this kind of case is important to the extent that political corruption occurs via interrelated networks of officeholders. This is a frequent feature of corruption in customs, where members of the corrupted networks tend to reinforce the corrupt practice by sharing the ensuing profits with colleagues and superiors, thus normalizing the practice within their institution (see, e.g., De Wulf and Sokol 2005). Our approach makes a salient characteristic of this kind of case visible: The border officers' corrupt conduct is an alteration of the normative order within which officeholders' institutional relations occur and make sense. It is in virtue of their being part of this normative order that the officeholders have the moral standing of asking each other to answer for the uses they make of their power of office with reference to that power mandate. When a corrupt institutional practice is established, this normative order ipso facto fails and individual officeholders lose their moral standing to call other officeholders out for their corrupt conduct. This is because they could not recall their colleagues to their duty of office accountability without a measure of hypocrisy. Both G. A. Cohen and Anthony Duff have remarked that holding someone accountable importantly requires some form of reciprocity, such that I cannot ask someone to give me an account of her failure to comply with a standard or a norm if I am not complying with that standard or norm in the first place (Duff 2018; Cohen 2006). We can expect that when political corruption occurs in an institutional practice, the agent who is called to answer for her conduct rejects the others' authority to demand a justification of her action because the others have failed to comply with the relevant norm themselves.[15] This consideration aptly emphasizes the relational dimension of the wrongness of political corruption proper of corrupt networks of officeholders. Our approach targets these corrupt networks upfront and, thus, sets a specific agenda for an anticorruption initiative aimed at restoring a just normative order of interactions instead.

In the next chapter, we consider the implications of our normative theory of the wrongness of political corruption for anticorruption policies. But the considerations we have just offered prompt some reflection on the prospective responsibilities for anticorruption that bear emphasizing here too. The relational nature of the wrong for which officeholders are held morally responsible in cases of political corruption makes the resort to punitive practices (of the kind "Those who cause a damage must pay for it") important and necessary, but also insufficient to attend to the demands of anticorruption. Of course, we recognize that punishment, apology, reparation, or removal from office may sometimes be the most appropriate answer to officeholders' corrupt conduct. However, only by examining particular cases is it possible to establish whether the appropriate answer to someone's responsibility for political corruption is dismissal or resignation from office. What bears emphasizing here is that those who are retrospectively responsible for political corruption are not always also the ones who are best positioned to take up anticorruption prospective responsibilities. In the example under discussion, it seems difficult, even if not impossible, to imagine that the corrupt border officers can reach by their own initiative a credible commitment to opposing political corruption without an external intervention capable of bringing

[15] The so-called "tu quoque" argument is aimed at defeating an opponent's claim by showing that the opponent has failed to comply with the moral standards underpinning that claim. Also known as an appeal to hypocrisy, it is a type of logical fallacy and may be considered a form of argumentum ad hominem. We are not committed to the general validity of this argument, which, however, seems a worthwhile consideration in the context of mutual accountability, which we are considering.

about a substantial institutional transformation. This predicament may be due to high peer pressure to maintain the corrupt network in place to salvage the privileges of sharing the profits that derive from a well-established network of personal connections, which sometimes also sees collusion with organized crime. A change of pace requires a structural transformation with better mechanisms of internal control or the appointment of new officials with a clean personal record. We suggest that what is crucial for such a transformation to occur is that, whatever action is taken, it calls the entire institution (as an interrelated structure of embodied roles) to action. In this sense, as we will see in Chapter 5, any such action is a matter of public ethics of office.

6. Responsibility for morphological political corruption

Morphological cases of political corruption occur when an officeholder behaves in a corrupt manner and, in virtue of the interrelatedness of institutional roles, makes it impossible for other officeholders to act in keeping with their power mandate, thus establishing a corrupt practice that fails the institution's raison d'être. In Chapter 2, we illustrated this case with reference to an officeholder, entrusted with the power of seeking scientific evidence on the dangers of a new pharmaceutical product, who receives a bribe to appoint an expert who can deliver a favorable scientific opinion. When the officeholders entrusted with the power to authorize the marketing of that pharmaceutical product base their decision on that report, the rationale of the entire procedure is compromised and we can say that the marketing authority has failed its raison d'être.

In cases like this one, we can clearly assign retrospective individual responsibility to the corrupt officeholder. He is morally responsible both for the end-state injustice that the corrupt practice is likely to generate (e.g., in terms of an unfair distribution of health-related risks for those who take the drug) and for the interactive injustice of the deficit of office accountability in the officeholder's conduct. To assign the officeholder retrospective responsibility for establishing the corrupt institutional practice is therefore appropriate, and so is holding him prospectively responsible by asking him to apologize and accept the punishment for his action. The responsibility of the other officeholders is harder to assess. They may have been totally unaware of their colleague's corrupt conduct and could, therefore, make a case that they have exercised their power of office for an agenda that, to the best of their knowledge, had a rationale coherent with the terms of their mandate. Nevertheless, the practice of marketing authorization is corrupt, and they took part in it. Is it appropriate to attribute retrospective responsibility to them for their colleague's corrupt conduct? Or for an institutional mechanism that they did not create? Should we simply consider them as blameless participants in a corrupt practice?

In morphological cases of political corruption too, we can attend to these questions from the perspective of the officeholders' interrelated responsibility for an interactive injustice. From this perspective, regardless of their causal or contributive role in establishing the corrupt institutional practice, all officeholders involved in that practice can be engaged to answer for its corruption. Retrospectively, the officeholders involved in the corrupt practice bear interrelated responsibility for the deficit of office accountability of the institutional practice in which they partake. To hold them responsible in this sense means to activate them to understand the interactive injustice that occurred within their institution and ask them to acknowledge the weakness of their interrelated work. This weakness consists in their interrelated action, which has failed their institution's raison d'être, for example by failing to be vigilant and uphold an appropriate institutional commitment or by identifying some important omissions whose rationale would not pass the test of office accountability.

We thus have a key for assigning retrospective responsibilities for political corruption to all officeholders as an institution. For example, officeholders may be called to answer for letting their corrupt colleague alone to face the pressure of powerful interest groups (such as the pharmaceutical industry). Of course, some officeholders could rejoin that it was in their colleague's remit to resist those pressures. Nevertheless, this line of reasoning seems capable of identifying objective difficulties in managing the relations with powerful actors external to the institution and an internal lack of supportive action aimed at preventing, stopping, or detecting political corruption and prioritizing office accountability. Notably, this lack can be a symptom of compromised institutional relations. The corrupt officeholder's colleagues have failed to hold him accountable for the use he was making of his power of office. In this sense, they share the interrelated responsibility for the interactive injustice that has thereby occurred. While none of the officeholders, by isolated action, could have prevented establishing the corrupt practice, they could have managed to do so as an institution.[16] In this sense, officeholders in their interrelatedness have come up short of their duty of office accountability. To hold officeholders interrelatedly responsible can facilitate understanding the wrongness of their conduct in their institutional capacity and activate them, in that capacity, to investigate their relational shortcomings in order to halt corrupt institutional practices and discourage their future occurrence.

By taking seriously the relational wrongness of their unaccountable interrelated action, officeholders are engaged in an exercise of public ethics in which they should consider their institutional relations and the rationale of the agenda pursued by their interrelated work in light of the raison d'être of their institution. This is an important call to prospective action because in morphological cases of political corruption the interrelated officeholders' failure to uphold

---

[16] For an illustration of this dynamic of interaction, see Feinberg (1970a).

the raison d'être of their institution is not always obvious. Bringing this failure to the fore is clearly, in most cases, an essential preliminary step in assuming responsibility and understanding how to design anticorruption initiatives. In this way, officeholders are normatively and practically engaged in the task of understanding how their institutional relations can be corrected, and the normative order of interactions governed by office accountability is restored.

Unlike the border officials in the summative-model example, in cases of morphologically corrupt institutional practices, political corruption is not instantiated in the individual conduct of each and every officeholder, even if as interrelated individuals they can be said to have failed to act in accordance with office accountability. The officeholders thus retain their moral standing to hold each other answerable for their conduct and, on that basis, to call on each other to take up prospective anticorruption responsibilities. In this context, individual officeholders can keep their institution faithful to its raison d'être only in cooperation with their fellow institutional members by addressing the institutional weakness that the identification of political corruption reveals and institutionalizing the commitment to anticorruption. By realizing the relational character of the wrongness of political corruption, officeholders may come to understand that anticorruption is not just a matter of individual morality but—as we extensively show in the next chapter—one of public ethics.

7. Responsibility for systemic corruption

Systemic corruption is the most recalcitrant form of political corruption in terms of assigning responsibility. Under systemic corruption, a plurality of institutions—including private and public organizations, possibly as well as criminal organizations or elites dominating the social life of a country—entertain a complex network of corrupt exchanges, typically over a long period of time. As discussed in Chapter 2, mapping this network is necessary to under-stand its constitutive relationships and possibly to disentangle the summative and morphological components of the corrupt system. In virtue of this complexity, distinguishing between the causes and effects of a corrupt system, ascertaining what sort of behavior has contributed to establishing that system, and thus pinpointing the specific causal responsibilities for the end-state injustices thereby produced, seems to be a daunting and hopeless task.

However, as already argued in the analysis of holding officeholders responsible for summatively and morphologically corrupt institutional practices, reconstruction of the causes and effects of political corruption and identification of the relative contributions of individual officeholders are neither the only nor the best ways to establish the normative sources of moral respon-sibility for political corruption. In our deontological approach, re-sponsibility for political corruption is assigned in consideration of the rationale of the agenda guiding an officeholder's action (rather than its consequences) or, in this specific case, her decision to par-ticipate in a corrupt system.

To see the advantage of our deontological approach, consider that—quite straightforwardly—in many cases of systemic cor-ruption, the decision of a single officeholder to refuse to adapt to a corrupt practice is insufficient to stop political corruption. In an institutional context of systemic bribery, for example, when citizens are expected to pay the relevant administrator to receive some public services (such as obtaining a document for their visa application) that should be free, even if one officeholder refused the bribe, the practice of bribing would not cease to exist. People claiming a service would continue to be treated as customers rather than as citizens. Thus, the causal contribution of the officeholder's participation in or withdrawal from maintaining the corrupt prac-tice is negligible. Single officeholders typically do not have control over systemic political corruption. Therefore, if we make moral re-sponsibility dependent on causal responsibility, we may be capable of assessing the officeholder's individual morality with respect to his specific conduct taken in isolation (has the officeholder taken a bribe?). But it is not clear what conclusions we could draw for assessing the officeholder's responsibility for the corrupt institutional practice (has the officeholder contributed to the maintenance of the practice of bribery within his institution?).

However, if we shift to our interactive-justice-based perspective, the evaluation of the officeholder's conduct does make a difference both for the assessment of his individual action (has the officeholder violated his duty of office accountability?) and for the ways he has performed his institutional role in its interrelation with those of his colleagues involved in the corrupt institutional practice (what actions has the officeholder taken to ensure that the powers of office in his organization are exercised in ways that can pass the test of office accountability?). In other words, from our perspective, officeholders who participate in corrupt institutional practices are not only answerable for their individual conduct—severally taken—and for the wrongful end-states thereby generated. In virtue of the interrelatedness of institutional roles, officeholders are also retrospectively responsible for the ways in which their conduct interplays with the conduct of their fellow role occupants and for the wrongful structure of institutional relations thus constituted. In this specific sense, we can thus say that any individual officeholder who partakes in a corrupt system can be held morally responsible for that interactive injustice irrespectively of the size, quality, and impact of her individual contributions to the wrong deriving from the joint work of "many hands."[17]

---

[17] A classic case study of the many hands phenomenon is the Italian judicial inquiry "Mani Pulite" (Della Porta and Vannucci 2007). The investigation started in 1992 with the arrest of the manager of a public hospital, Mario Chiesa, and expanded to reach thousands of politicians, bureaucrats, and entrepreneurs who were involved in various forms of political corruption. In a couple of years, it produced a scandal that led to a dramatic crisis in the Italian party system. In this system, political corruption was practiced and justified by arguing that democratic competition requires material resources that can be ensured only through an established system of clientelism. In this system, individual officeholders did not even have the perception of committing a crime, but only of

So far we have shown how our deontological approach to establishing officeholders' responsibilities in cases of systemic corruption can work retrospectively. One may still challenge it on prospective grounds. For example, recall the institutionalists' important concern that the practice of holding officeholders responsible for systemic corruption is likely to lead to either finding scapegoats or holding everybody indistinctively responsible (see also Thompson 1980, 906). This concern voices the consideration that, while in looking retrospectively at systemic corruption we may identify instances of blameworthy conduct among officeholders, we cannot reasonably hope to solve the problem of systemic corruption solely by discarding the "bad apples" thus identified. A related risk is that the practice of holding individual officeholders answerable for systemic corruption translates into a "witch hunt," whereby many individuals are (more or less rightly) excluded from public office. This condition may result, in turn, in a dispersion of skills, experiences, and commitments that could instead be capitalized on for improving the functioning of the institution and countering the corruption of its practices. Think, for example, of countries where the national health care system is tainted by a structure of nursing homes and hospitals where a complex scheme of bribes and clientelism has come to govern the patients' admission and treatment. The scheme is so pervasive that as a large part of the medical staff in the country is implicated in one way or another; doctors tend to favor members from their personal networks in managing the waiting lists, and nurses frequently receive gifts in exchange for their services to specific patients. Moreover, even those employees who do not have a direct role are implicated as they turn a blind eye

following the necessities of party politics and the logic of political competition. During the trials, many defendants pointed out as an exculpatory element that they could not be singled out to be responsible for establishing the clientelist system and that they only played by the game.

to their colleagues' conduct.[18] If these cases of systemic corruption were tackled only by a strategy of detecting and removing the "bad apples" (meaning, in this case, dismissing all members of the medical staff actually responsible for taking bribes or other forms of misconduct), the health care system itself would cease to function (or even exist) and the more pervasive aspects of political corruption (e.g., the silence surrounding it) would remain intact.

Even more worrying for some institutionalists is the risk related to assigning collective responsibility for systemic corruption; the risk consists in the prospect of criminalizing retrospectively all those involved in the corrupt institution irrespectively of their actual standing within it or their motives. In addition, collective punishment is disappointing prospectively, too, because it may not even bring about the expected changes in the corrupt system. Here the institutionalists' preoccupation is with the possibility that, even if there is a change in the specific persons who occupy some institutional roles, the corrupt institutional structure may remain in place and, therefore, easily relapse into corruption. Networks of clientelism, for one, are often too entrenched and deep-seated to be discarded by removing certain corrupt individuals, as the preexisting institutional structures and incentives for corruption (perhaps under the influence of criminal organizations) tend to survive and return.

We think these institutionalists' concerns are warranted, but they are raised for the wrong reasons. These concerns are warranted because, indeed, merely punitive responses to political corruption do not seem capable of dissolving the corrupt institutional relationships entrenched in systemically corrupt institutional practices. We have seen this aspect in our discussion of the corrupt health system in the earlier example. Of course, as already argued, some forms of punishing or sanctioning the corrupt behavior of

---

[18] Recent data show that this situation is particularly troublesome in countries such as Croatia, Greece, Lithuania, Hungary, Poland, and Romania (see EC 2017).

individual doctors and nurses can be the appropriate answers to their individual violations of office accountability (as their power mandate certainly does not include helping friends or providing services on the basis of the patients' generosity). We view the appropriateness of this reaction as an entirely deontological matter that depends on the structure of the wrongdoing that thereby occurs and is, in this sense, independent of the actual or expected institutional changes such measures may bring about. There is, however, a sense in which assigning officeholders individual retrospective responsibilities for systemic corruption may be functional to understand where the wrongful dynamics of officeholders' interaction are located. Such an understanding is, we argue, a necessary step in engaging officeholders to take prospective action for restoring just institutional relations.

Our approach suggests, more generally, that holding officeholders individually and interrelatedly responsible for systemic corruption involves reminding all the parties (those directly implicated in the corrupt practices as well as those who more or less turn a blind eye to such practices) of what is required of an institutional role occupant when she exercises her power of office. Pointing at the deficits of office accountability in the officeholders' conduct can make officeholders aware of the inherent wrongness of their conduct. Gaining this awareness is essential to undermine the faulty rationalizations of an officeholder's own corruption typical of those operations of redescription of an officeholder's conduct, which we illustrated in Chapter 1 and on which systemic corruption trades.[19] Because of these operations, bribes become tokens of appreciation for services rendered, and clientelism is coated in the terminology of solidarity. Bringing the untenability of these operations to light is one important achievement of our approach in terms of prospective anticorruption. Moreover, in such cases of systemic corruption

---

[19] For an extensive discussion of individual tainted rationalizations under systemic corruption, see Ceva and Radoilska (2018).

as that instantiated in the corrupt health care system, when a certain corrupt line of action is widespread and its occurrence is regular, individual corrupt conduct tends to be normalized. Fostering the officeholders' awareness of their own corruption is an important way to resist this normalization and is, therefore, a further important achievement of the practice of assigning retrospective responsibility for systemic corruption.

Relatedly, assignment of retrospective responsibility for systemic corruption is useful to counter *generalized* rationalizations of corrupt practices—such as, for example, an overexcusatory rhetoric—and to recall officeholders to the raison d'être of the institution within which they operate. Resorting to claims of "Everybody does it" vis-à-vis charges of political corruption may work as an excuse if we consider the wrongness of political corruption through the lens of individual contributions to the generation of an end-state injustice. Indeed, in the context of systemic corruption, the large number of wrongdoers may dilute the proportion of individual contributions to the final damage caused by the corrupt practice. But, as already suggested, if we consider an officeholder's conduct from the deontological point of view of the rationale of the agenda she pursues, we can identify a deficit of office accountability for which the officeholder retains full moral responsibility. Similarly, self-deceptive ways of explaining away political corruption by referring to an alleged demand to adapt to "the system" can be contrasted by the practice of calling officeholders to respond for the rationale of the agenda they pursue by their power of office.

Finally, officeholders' awareness of their retrospective responsibility for systemic corruption is an apparent necessary step for them to entertain an anticorruption commitment. It is hard to imagine that any progress toward restoring interactive justice in the earlier-mentioned case of a corrupt health care system can be initiated and pursued unless the various members of the medical staff understand—each of them in their own specific role-related way—the wrongness of the practice that implicates them and accept responsibility for it. In such cases, the depth and breadth of corrupt dynamics of officeholders' interaction are such that they require a structural change from within that involves the largest possible number of (directly and indirectly) implicated agents. Anticorruption may not unilaterally come from above (say, from the ministry of health) or, in fact, outside of a systemically corrupt institution (e.g., by the sole intervention of the judiciary). The systemic character of political corruption calls for an equally systemic anticorruption initiative. This is the sense in which we want to read the claim that anticorruption must find "cultural entry points" in order to create virtuous circles leading to institutional well-functioning. We have given reasons to those who hold this view to recognize that the officeholders' taking responsibility for systemic corruption is a necessary step toward any significant cultural change in the organizational culture. To the extent that political corruption is morally excused because it is not predicated on responsible human agents, but on an impersonal "system" or an external authority, it is difficult to imagine where the impulse toward a positive cultural anticorruption development could come from.

Being grounded in a public ethics of office, our approach to assessing political corruption is demanding. However, this consideration should not suggest that we adopt a hypermoralized approach to the normative assessment of an officeholder's conduct. Surely, the kind of conduct that we can expect of an officeholder who acts within a well-functioning institution is different from that reasonably required of those who hold an institutional role within a corrupt institution. The personal costs of individual noncompliance with a corrupt institutional practice may be very high and involve both the officeholder's professional and personal lives (e.g., defection may curtail the officeholder's career and her relations with her colleagues) and those of her dependents (e.g., they may suffer from the loss of the defecting officeholder's job). Moreover, as remarked in our discussion of the morphological model of political corruption, it is very difficult for an individual officeholder always to act in accountable ways when some of her colleagues are corrupt. In virtue of the interrelatedness of institutional roles, one or more officeholders may be prevented from acting in an accountable way because someone else has altered the institutional practice in which they are engaged (e.g., by accepting a bribe to seek vitiated scientific evidence on which an institutional decision will subsequently be based).

Operating in a public institution whose constitutive relations are disrupted by political corruption makes it more difficult for individual officeholders to fulfill their duty of office accountability. Very often, public institutions affected by systemic corruption fail to provide structures that allow for practices of answerability, for example, by promoting the officeholders' mutual support and counseling. Even when some answerability practices are in place, where there is a deficit of office accountability in institutional relations, the actual expectations concerning the officeholders' conduct and the basis for mutual trust are distorted and undermined. Restoring just institutional relations requires that officeholders in that institution make an extra effort. This includes newly appointed officeholders who may have in no way causally contributed to compromising those relations and who may be willing, for example, to promote reforms and practices to strengthen relations of accountability. Nevertheless, it is an implication of our argument that all officeholders (old and new) can be equally called upon to resist political corruption and take restorative steps to ensure the establishment of just institutional relations. To do so, we contend, prospective responsibility for political corruption cannot be conceived as a mere matter of an officeholder's personal ethics of complying with her professional obligations. More significantly, it is a matter of public ethics of the officeholders who operate in their interrelatedness as an institution governed by deontic relations of office accountability. As we discuss in the next chapter, an officeholder's anticorruption obligations are not exhausted in his individual conscientious refusal to adapt to a corrupt institutional practice. Anticorruption requires that an officeholder assume the interrelated responsibility for how his institution operates.

The difficulties that an individual officeholder may encounter to keep her conduct faithful to her power mandate in the context of systemic corruption allow us to add two further considerations to our argument in this section. First, to say that officeholders are bound by a *duty* of office accountability nevertheless leaves us the space to praise the conduct of those officeholders who manage to act on that duty in the context of systemic corruption (despite their personal costs). Second, the moral assessment of an officeholder's conduct in terms of the interrelated responsibility for systemic corruption is not primarily meant either as a retrospective judgment of personal morality (aimed to establish an officeholder's corrupt character) or as a prospective call to individual action (which might be too costly or just impossible in the circumstances). Rather, it aims retrospectively at disentangling the structural relationship dynamics that, in virtue of the interrelatedness of institutional roles, constitute a systemically corrupt practice. Moreover, it calls prospectively for institutional anticorruption action. In other words, this conclusion reinforces our claim that holding officeholders responsible for political corruption is a matter of *public* ethics.

8. Conclusion

In this chapter, we have argued that establishing moral responsibility for individual corrupt conduct and for corrupt institutional practices is best understood as a set of practices of answerability within a public ethics of office accountability. We have specified the kind of wrong for which officeholders may be considered individually or interrelatedly blameworthy in the relational terms of an interactive injustice. Assigning responsibility for political corruption as a relational kind of wrong brings out the salience of the interrelatedness of the officeholders' conduct both in becoming agents of political corruption and in taking up prospective responsibility to restore the normative order of interactions that political corruption disrupts.

We have shown that our account of the wrongness of political corruption as an interactive injustice reveals how officeholders may be held responsible for political corruption even when it is difficult to disentangle their individual causal contributions to the establishment and maintenance of a corrupt institutional practice or some end-state injustice. Moreover, we have argued that—in virtue of the interrelatedness of their institutional roles—officeholders can take interrelated responsibility for the wrongness of an institution's failure to remain faithful to its raison d'être in virtue of the corrupt relations among its members. The idea of assigning officeholders interrelated responsibility for political corruption is not to hold them blameworthy simply for being part of an institution, but rather to engage them in an institutional communicative practice revealing morally troublesome deficits of office accountability, with a view to addressing those deficits through institutional action in a restorative perspective.

To hold officeholders responsible for political corruption thus allows us to gain a better understanding of the injustice of political corruption as nested in institutional structures. Such an understanding of the interactive injustice of political corruption is preliminary to identifying appropriate ways to correct disrupted institutional relations and promote just relations in their stead. This exercise is primarily internal to a public institution and concerns the exercise of the officeholders' duties of office and their interrelated understanding of their power mandate and institutional action. So conceived, as we show in the next chapter, anticorruption pertains to the domain of a public ethics of office, rather than exclusively to the sphere of the officeholder's personal morality or the domain of legal justice.

5

Opposing political corruption

1. Introduction

This chapter brings into focus how the components of a public ethics of office accountability can guide officeholders in opposing political corruption. The fallibility of human action and the interrelatedness of institutional roles explain how political corruption is always a threat even for well-designed public institutions. Political corruption occurs when officeholders use the powers entrusted to their institutional roles to pursue an agenda whose rationale may not be vindicated as coherent with the terms of their power mandate. We have explained how this form of corruption is inherently wrong as a deficit of office accountability in a broadly legitimate or nearly just public institutional setting. Because public institutions are *interrelated* systems of embodied roles, the corruption of the officeholders' conduct translates into corrupt institutional practices. In this sense, we have submitted that political corruption is an internal enemy of public institutions and, as such, an object of public ethics in its own right.

We build on this analytical and normative characterization of political corruption to flesh out what it takes for a public institution, as a system of interrelated agents, to oppose political corruption. Rather than providing a list of best practices, we point out how the officeholders should activate from within their institution the sort of practices that can uphold a public ethics of office accountability. That such practices come from within a public institution is important because we conceive the source of political corruption and its wrongness as internal to the institution. Therefore, the

Political Corruption. Emanuela Ceva and Maria Paola Ferretti, Oxford University Press (2021). © Oxford University Press. DOI: 10.1093/oso/9780197567869.003.0006

most significant actions to oppose political corruption must also come from within a public institution and mobilize, above all, the officeholders. These actions may not be left entirely to third-parties (e.g., an anticorruption authority or some supervisory body).

To oppose political corruption is irreducible to engaging in anticorruption legal and regulatory actions, but anticorruption should be understood as a component of a public ethics of office accountability. In what follows, we show how anticorruption is the name appropriately used to describe those practices by which a public institution should respond to internal deficits of office accountability. These practices, as we will explain, are justified by the officeholders' obligations to restore the interactively just institutional relations that political corruption constitutively disrupts.

We start in §2 by clarifying the specific function of anticorruption but, also, to integrate it within the broader framework of a public ethics of office accountability. To achieve this aim, we take some steps backward to flesh out the main components of this public ethics, spell out the duties they generate for officeholders (§3 and 4), and situate in that respect the implications for officeholders' anticorruption obligations (§5). In this way, we should be able to preserve the particularity of anticorruption (as a response to the particular kind of institutional wrongdoing in which this form of unaccountable use of entrusted power consists), without reducing it to a series of ad hoc measures. Anticorruption is, rather, conceived as an integral part of what it takes and means for a public institution to be well-functioning and, therefore, oppose political corruption from within.

2. Anticorruption: too narrow or too broad?

Current approaches to anticorruption have been either narrowly circumscribed to regulatory or punitive actions or broadly inclusive of policies aimed at enhancing an institution's functioning and organizational culture. On the first count, anticorruption has been conceived as a retributive mechanism primarily meant to point out and censor officeholders' corrupt conduct (by legally prosecuting and punishing corrupt officeholders or removing them from office).[1] But anticorruption has also included preemptive interventions aimed at restricting the margins of officeholders' discretion to reduce arbitrary abuses of power. [2] On the second count, anticorruption is characterized as a response to the limits of legalistic claims to repair the damages of political corruption. Therefore, a broader set of initiatives has been championed to promote a more ethical behavior among officeholders and good institutional practices. [3] These initiatives include under the umbrella term of *anticorruption* such an array of instruments as organizational codes of conduct, transparency mechanisms, and whistleblowing.

A more encompassing approach to anticorruption may be helpful to overcome the strictures of a retributive—mainly legalistic—and regulatory institutional response to political corruption. However, we are also concerned that it risks turning the focus and mission of anticorruption from too narrow to too broad, thus losing the specificity necessary to target the institutional responses to political

---

[1] Criminal prosecution is still considered one of the core tools for fighting corruption across national and supranational institutions. For example, one of the major innovations introduced in the European Anti-Fraud Office's (OLAF) anticorruption strategy is the establishment of a European Public Prosecutors Office (EPPO). Since the end of 2020, EPPO has been entrusted with the task of carrying out cross-border criminal investigations and prosecutions (https://ec.europa.eu/info/law/cross-border-cases/judicial-cooperation/networks-and-bodies-supporting-judicial-cooperation/european-public-prosecutors-office_en).

[2] Abuse of officeholders' discretion is considered one of the main types of corruption in the *UN Guide for Anti-Corruption Policies* prepared by the UN Office on Drugs and Crime (2003). Conversely, the *Guide* explicitly mentions the regulation of official discretion as one of the institutional reforms key to curbing corruption (https://www.unodc.org/pdf/crime/corruption/UN_Guide.pdf).

[3] Many international bodies engaged in the fight against political corruption have emphasized the centrality of overcoming a purely administrative approach and developing a "mentality of anticorruption" (see, e.g., the 2010 UNDP Report on *Fighting Corruption in Post-conflict and Recovery Situations: Learning from the Past* (http://content-ext.undp.org/aplaws_publications/2594849/Fighting%20corruption%20in%20post-conflict%20and%20recovery%20situations.pdf).

corruption. So, we think it is important to avoid the Scylla of the reductivist strictures of the retributive and regulatory approach, but we should also be careful to stand clear of the Charybdis of the overinclusion of its critical counterpart—while we should cater to respond to the main preoccupations of both approaches.

Let us start by looking more closely at the mainstream and most established approach to anticorruption. A legalistic approach to anticorruption that revolves around the punishment of corrupt public officials may consist of retributive practices. From a retributive perspective, punishment is characteristically condemnatory, and so it seems an appropriate instance of anticorruption as a legal reaction to political corruption. Under other understandings, punishment (and penalties in general) have the additional function of creating disincentives for corrupt behavior or rehabilitating corrupt offenders (see Feinberg 1970b and, for a general discussion, Duff 2017). Retributive practices concern the just treatment of the perpetrator of some wrongdoing (Murphy 2017, 84). For retributivists, this just treatment requires a response of proportional punishment. Depending on the offense, anticorruption measures may include the corrupt officeholder's removal from his job; his professional demotion; or his imprisonment—in the case of criminal offenses such as bribery or misappropriation.

Moreover, legal anticorruption measures may take the form of corrective practices. Corrective practices concentrate on the just response to wrongful losses suffered by the victims. The central claim here is that victims should be "repaired" (Murphy 2017, 96–97). This reparation typically includes some form of compensation that makes victims "whole" by putting them in a position they would have been in had the wrong not occurred. Compensations for victims of political corruption could be monetary (including the restitution of ill-gotten gains) or could involve other forms of repair such as reopening a job opportunity that was vitiated by a nepotistic hiring practice.

The legalistic approach to anticorruption is quite clearly animated by a predominant retrospective concern; but it also incorporates prospective measures because it may generate new responsibilities for the offenders (concerning, for example, the compensation of victims) or aim at creating disincentives for corruption (e.g., by fear of punishment). Moreover, legal action may also include preventive measures such as stricter regulation of the terms of exercise of the power of office. Typically, these regulatory anticorruption measures tend to reduce the amount of discretion and the margins for personal maneuver, which officeholders may abuse, thus generating political corruption.

These legalistic measures are undeniably important and can easily be recognized in many national and international anticorruption initiatives. Insofar as the corrupt conduct of an officeholder can be identified or her causal contribution to establishing a corrupt institutional practice can be circumscribed and quantified, retributive and corrective anticorruption practices are warranted. But there are a few buts.

For a starter, prospective legal anticorruption action may simply not be viable if it is premised on a retrospective causal or contributive approach to the assignment of responsibilities for political corruption. As seen in Chapter 4, in many instances of political corruption (notably but not exclusively in systemic cases), the reconstruction of the causal chain that has led to establishing a corrupt practice looks tantalizing. Efforts to design just, effective, and efficient retributive and compensatory measures may therefore seem doomed and at risk of fostering practices of scapegoating or witch hunting. By making retributive actions central, this approach conceives of anticorruption as such as a punitive answer to retrospective officeholders' causal or contributive responsibilities for political corruption. But such responsibilities are not always assessable, especially when they concern the contributions of many individuals to a corrupt institutional practice. Therefore, retributive anticorruption strategies run the risk of incentivizing scapegoating. This risk materializes, for example, when the main reaction to such corruption scandals as those involving bribery leads to an investigation aimed at singling out who received what from whom. As seen in the case of the corrupt system surrounding the construction of the Willy Brand Airport, this strategy runs the risk of identifying anticorruption with the criminal prosecution and exemplary punishment of a small portion of the individuals involved, typically those whose misconduct can be easily discovered and proved. This approach tends to leave out from the investigation other officeholders who in different ways made that misconduct possible and who are thus dispensed for taking responsibility for the corruption of the system. The same tendency can be observed, for instance, with reference to practices of money smuggling within border control agencies. These are just a couple of additional examples of political corruption that, as discussed in the previous chapters, see the involvement of the "many hands" of various officeholders at different levels of more or less advertent participation in corrupt institutional practices.

Obviously, a number of moral and practical problems are involved in identifying anticorruption with the practice of scapegoating. In a first sense, it may be used merely as a rhetorical move to mimic the intention of opposing political corruption, without in fact taking any meaningful action to understand and address it. Moreover, scapegoating can be maliciously used in politics—for example, when allegations of political corruption become a powerful weapon for punishing (or weakening the credibility of) political adversaries, or when they are instrumentally used as the basis for removing from office noncompliant officeholders. In these cases, punitive anticorruption initiatives can easily be used as an expedient for gaining and mastering political advantage rather than for addressing and opposing political corruption at all.[4]

---

[4] The charges of a "clockwork" use of justice for political purposes have been an integral part of the claims of such right-wing leaders as Donald Trump in the United States and Silvio Berlusconi in Italy, as they were investigated for abuses of power and bribery

Notice also that, for some commentators, an entirely legalistic perspective is wanting because it implies a troubling measure of "moral minimalism," as it cannot capture instances of political corruption in which officeholders act in a corrupt way without, however, breaking any law (Jennings 1995). This is frequently the case vis-à-vis instances of nepotism or familism, which are not always outlawed and whose occurrence is sometimes hard to ascertain. On the other hand, the countertendency to this minimalism is overregulation, with the aim of restricting room for officeholders' discretion. Even if the intention of a more dense regulation is to describe precisely what kinds of conduct are prohibited, an overly regulatory tendency risks stigmatizing any use of officeholders' discretion. This happens, for example, when rules are introduced that exclude as eligible candidates for a post in a public office those who are related (even remotely) to people currently employed in the same office.[5] As we already discussed in Chapter 1, officeholders' discretion is an important feature of the uses of a power of office in order to avoid turning officeholders into mere executors of the mechanical application of rules. An officeholder's tasks must be performed, we have seen, within significant margins for the exercise of her judgment and the ability to discriminate between different cases to which the rules relevant for any one of her tasks may apply.

When the margins for an officeholder's discretion are (sometimes dramatically) reduced, we risk the paralysis of institutional action, which typically involves the implementation of cumbersome proceedings for monitoring and enforcing the application of this (over)regulation. For example, this drawback of an overregulatory

during their electoral campaigns of 2016 and 2013, respectively. For a discussion of the Italian case, see, for example, Sberna and Vannucci (2013).

[5] This is the case, for example, of the Italian law on university recruitment, which excludes candidates up to the fourth degree of kinship (art. 18, Law 240, 30/12/2010, https://www.altalex.com/documents/leggi/2014/09/24/universita-la-riforma-gelmini-e-legge#art18).

approach to anticorruption can be seen at the root of a proliferation of complex technicalities and intricate procedures in such domains subject to public regulation as that of urban planning, concerning, for example, the rules for changing the designated use of certain urban areas, as well as the allocation of development rights. These complexities and intricacies have often been viewed as setting the circumstances for political corruption, for instance, in the form of bribes for breaking the inertia of some cumbersome authorization mechanisms whose rationale is not endorsed by officeholders but is perceived as a coercive intrusion (see, e.g., Chiodelli 2019 and Chiodelli and Moroni 2015).

Finally, the most powerful argument against excessive reductions of office discretion is probably that enforcing legality in an overregulated system is very cumbersome for the judiciary. Excessive workload, the courts' lack of resources for dealing with all alleged cases of political corruption, and the slow pace of legal procedures often result in a backlog of cases or the failure to prosecute political corruption at all. The unwanted, paradoxical effect is that, in this way, the legalistic approach may hinder rather than foster legal anticorruption action.

These practical considerations help us to appreciate the importance of establishing officeholders' prospective responsibilities independently of their retrospective contribution to political corruption that we defended in Chapter 4. When anticorruption measures are handed mainly to the intervention of third parties (e.g., some anticorruption governmental authority or the judiciary), they underplay the prospective responsibilities that pertain to officeholders and their duty to take direct first-personal action to prevent political corruption from occurring again in the future of their institution.[6] Officeholders are called to assume

---

[6] These and other criticalities concerning the implementation of an anticorruption strategy that draws primarily on the legal action of third parties are central to the assessments of efforts to oppose the corruption of political elites in such highly politicized judicial contexts as those in Uganda, for example (https://www.hrw.org/report/2013/10/21/letting-big-fish-swim/failures-prosecute-high-level-corruption-uganda) and Ukraine

this responsibility as a matter of interrelated responsibility, rather than on the basis of their individual retrospective responsibilities severally taken.

A further limit of retributive and corrective anticorruption practices is theoretical. Besides their potential practical drawbacks, these practices only voice demands of end-state justice. Just legal end-states are those in which corrupt officeholders are either removed from office or, in fact, proportionally punished for their corrupt conduct or involvement in corrupt institutional practices, and those who have been damaged by their corruption are appropriately repaired. However, there is also an interactive crucial and constitutive dimension to the injustice of political corruption, which the legalistic approaches have unwarrantedly overlooked. When we see the wrongness of political corruption in the relational terms of an interactive injustice, anticorruption cannot be limited to a negative remedial legal strategy to address the damages that corrupt officeholders and institutional practices cause. Anticorruption should, rather, be guided by a positive vision of what the opposite of political corruption is: A public institutional system that realizes office accountability. To this end, anticorruption must not only be punitive or discouraging of wrongful action; as we argue later, but must also be designed to provide positive guidance for officeholders to restore interactive justice by remedying the deficits of office accountability in which political corruption consists. It is in this sense that we suggest that anticorruption is one component of what it takes for a public institution to oppose political corruption by the officeholders' direct engagement.

This positive aspiration can be seen as lying beneath many attacks on the appropriateness of current anticorruption legalistic measures. These attacks have built on the earlier-mentioned criticisms and insist that anticorruption must have in fact a number

(https://www.chathamhouse.org/publication/are-ukraines-anti-corruption-reforms-working/2018-11-19-ukraine-anti-corruption-reforms-lough-dubrovskiy.pdf).

of entry points irreducible to a "top-down," mainly legalistic, retributive, and regulatory approach. Such an approach is wanting because, first and apparently, it only targets and counters those forms of political corruption that involve formal rule breaking (e.g., bribery but not necessarily nepotism). This restriction is problematic because it overlooks other, subtler but lawful forms of political corruption (as in the case of private electoral-campaign financing) and reduces political corruption to its symptoms (the bribe) without diagnosing and addressing the deeper illness (a system that incentivizes bribery as a form of doing business). From this point of view, anticorruption should be seen, more broadly, as a matter of analyzing and reforming the organizational culture of a public institution through a more complex system of policies that can promote a "more ethical" institutional conduct.

The need to promote a more encompassing and nuanced anticorruption agenda is not only an intellectual desideratum; it has been widely recognized by anticorruption activists too. For example, a recent report of the Council of Europe indicates that anticorruption is the cornerstone of the rule of law and a healthy democratic society, whose implementation requires complex sociopolitical action to promote good practices of institutional transparency, answerability, and civic education. Also, on October 19, 2016, the Congress of Local and Regional Authorities of the Council of Europe adopted a Road Map of Activities for promoting good anticorruption institutional practices at local and regional levels. This road map includes a varied set of practices ranging from gaining a better understanding of the risks of political corruption through preparing thematic reports (on, for instance, electoral resources, nepotism, and whistleblowing); the revision and extension of the scope of the European Code of Conduct; and the implementation of cooperation activities.

We welcome this forward-looking critical approach to retributive anticorruption strategies, and we particularly endorse the ethical turns it advocates. However, we think that equating anticorruption with the promotion of an ethical conduct tout court may stretch too much the focus of anticorruption as such. For example, organizational codes of conduct concern many aspects of the working environment and provide, quite typically, guidance for officeholders to avoid wrongful conduct, including theft, negligence, and—inter alia—corruption. The risk we see is to be left with too generic a set of instruments, which may result in misfiring by targeting too many different phenomena at once. An important—and related—consideration is the risk that the association of many of these important instruments (as organizational codes of conduct) with "anticorruption" may create a certain institutional resistance to adopt them as a way to fend off the accusation of being home to corruption.

Because we recognize the importance of these measures as well as the need to give specific content to anticorruption, we suggest that there is a currently underappreciated need to develop a more nuanced approach to opposing political corruption and, thus, offering purposeful guidance to the officeholders' action in their institutional capacity. Such an approach is premised on laying out the various duties that accrue to officeholders whose fulfillment is necessary for a public institution to be well-functioning, resist political corruption, but also be capable of detecting it and responding to it when it nevertheless occurs. This normative typology elucidates, in this book's parlance, the components of a public ethics of office accountability.

3. Standing clear of political corruption

A primary sense in which public institutions can oppose political corruption is that the officeholders in those institutions stand clear of political corruption. This statement may seem obvious, but it proves more interesting when we consider the great effort that anticorruption scholars and practitioners have devoted to devising institutional mechanisms for preventing, controlling, and finding remedies for political corruption. Less attention has been devoted to the idea that public institutions are not only made of rules and mechanisms, but above all of interrelated embodied roles. Paying attention to this idea means coming to see the opposition to political corruption not just as a procedural exercise of institutional-roles regulation, but as a matter of substantial public ethics that concerns the conduct of the human beings who occupy those roles. By refocusing attention on how the power attached to institutional roles is *exercised*, our main positive contribution in this book is to understand political corruption within the framework of a public ethics of office accountability.

Throughout this book, we have discussed what we consider the public ethics of office accountability should be for guiding officeholders' uses of their powers of office when they act in their institutional capacity. From the perspective of this public ethics, a just institutional system is one that instantiates just deontic institutional role-based relations between those who give body to those roles. These relations occur in forms of interaction between officeholders who mutually honor their normative status as occupants of institutional roles by exercising their powers of office in pursuit of an agenda whose rationale may be vindicated as coherent with the terms of their power mandate. In this way, through their interrelated action, officeholders uphold a normative order of interactions governed by office accountability. In our terminology, an institutional system that realizes this public ethics of office accountability is interactively just.

Within the framework of this public ethics of office, we have introduced the officeholders' primary duty of office accountability as a duty of interactive justice. As seen in Chapter 3, when someone assumes an institutional role, he acquires ipso facto a positive relational duty to use the powers entrusted to his role in pursuit of an agenda whose rationale may be vindicated as coherent with the terms of his power mandate. Because political corruption is a deficit of office accountability in this sense, it is an interactive injustice.

Therefore, officeholders also have a negative duty of office to stand clear of political corruption. This negative side of the duty of office accountability implies that officeholders are morally (not only legally) required not to engage in corrupt conduct or to participate in corrupt institutional practices. Like its positive counterpart, this negative duty is a deontic requirement whose validity is independent from consideration of the actual or expected consequences of an officeholder's action. As already discussed, under certain circumstances, the consideration of certain consequences may provide an excuse for the officeholder's implication in political corruption—for example, in dirty-hands scenarios or when it promotes an end-state justice. This excuse does not, however, detract from the presumptive wrongness of unaccountable institutional relations as a form of interactive injustice.

The condition that officeholders fulfill their duty of office accountability (both positively and negatively) is paramount from the perspective of a public ethics of office because it is critical to ensuring that a public institution is well-functioning. Thus, office accountability is primarily a regulative principle of an officeholder's conduct. Internalizing such a principle means recognizing its prescriptions as a guide for one's own behavior in one's institutional capacity. But we have also seen that an officeholder's duty of office accountability must be understood as one of the components of a public ethics of office, and it is thus irreducible to a series of practical guidelines for individual professional conduct. This consideration points to the relevance of the institutional environment for an officeholder's action. To fulfill the officeholders' duty to stand clear of political corruption as the interrelated members of a public institution means—among other things—to contribute to and maintain an institutional environment favorable to ensuring that powers of office are exercised in an accountable manner. In particular, institutional practices must be established that can foster the officeholders' awareness of what fulfilling the duty of office accountability requires.

Examples of institutional practices aimed to enhance the officeholders' awareness of their conduct are organizational codes of ethics. These codes of conduct are often a medium through which the officeholders can publicly express their commitment to uphold certain institutional practical guidelines and the interpretation of some institutional values (as, e.g., fairness or transparency). But most importantly, these codes can be a way for individual officeholders to communicate to each other (and thus raise their reciprocal awareness of) their willingness to follow those guidelines and to embrace those values as a way to fulfill their duty of office accountability as they perform their specific institutional functions. This awareness-enhancing function is corroborated by the results of some recent studies that have shown how the introduction of organizational codes of ethical conduct tends to promote compliancy, rather than simply increasing the identification of wrongdoing within institutions.[7] These results are significantly different from those discussed in many reports about the introduction of stricter legal regulations of office discretion, which is normally accompanied by increased reporting of wrongdoing in the absence of corresponding reductions in corrupt behaviors (Lambsdorff 2009). This contrast seems to support the hypothesis that organizational codes of ethical conduct can help create a supportive institutional environment for office accountability.

We should also mention those strategies aimed at offering more direct support to officeholders in discharging their duty of office accountability by identifying, for example, corruption pressure points through programs of corruption risk management. Such programs may include strategies for locating the roles that are most vulnerable to political corruption such as bribery, or for monitoring key junctures where officeholders are required to make concrete decisions that, by their nature, may be at risk of political corruption. This is frequently the case in health care or other public

---

[7] For a discussion and some data, see Somers (2001).

sectors charged with the realization of infrastructures, which are likely to be under pressure as they attract sizeable financial private interests or concern decisions that call on the officeholders' discretion to set priorities. Identifying and mapping the roles and key junctures most exposed to the risk of political corruption can be the first step in implementing specific measures to oppose political corruption from within a public institution. For example, such measures may include adopting a "rotation principle" to relieve and support the work of the occupants of those institutional positions at high risk of corruption; including disclosure and other information requirements in contracts and agreements in those areas where the occurrence of political corruption is expected; or else closely reviewing and oversighting protocols regarding the making of key decisions.

In summary, the first and most important way to oppose political corruption requires upholding the officeholder's duty to stand clear of it and their commitment to working in interrelatedness to create and maintain an institutional environment that is supportive of office accountability.

4. Detecting political corruption

After describing the officeholders' duty to stand clear of political corruption, we turn now to a discussion of a further component of our account of public ethics, which becomes relevant anytime officeholders suspect a deficit of office accountability within their institution. This component consists in a secondary duty that officeholders have to participate in answerability practices. As discussed in Chapter 4, the officeholders' responsibility for anticorruption includes a positive duty to respond in good faith to the questioning of their conduct in their institutional capacity. Discharging this duty requires that officeholders be ready to engage in practices of answerability aimed at establishing their retrospective and prospective, individual and interrelated, responsibilities for political corruption.

To focus on this further component reveals not only how officeholders have a duty to use, in the first person, their powers of office in keeping with the requirements of office accountability. They also have a (second personal) duty to engage in practices of reciprocal control of their institutional action. This duty is part of what is required of officeholders to uphold by their conduct the raison d'être of their institution, thus making their institution well-functioning by their interrelated action. Focusing on the pattern of the officeholders' interrelated action is of critical importance because, as seen in Chapter 2, it may be enough that any one officeholder comes up short of her duties of office for institutional dynamics to be set into motion that make by themselves a public institution fail its raison d'être. It is therefore necessary that officeholders also be constantly vigilant of the other officeholders' conduct.

To illustrate, consider "whistleblowing," the practice of reporting some alleged organizational wrongdoing by the member of an organization who has access to information concerning such wrongdoing.[8] Whistleblowing is a case in point of what an answerability practice should look like from our perspective. This practice was originally introduced in the domain of business ethics and corporate social responsibility to indicate the act of revealing information about a safety hazard present in the development of an artifact. However, its scope has steadily expanded and has now come to stand for an individual officeholder's extrema ratio against some grave organizational wrongdoing facing the failure of standard institutional checks and corrective measures.[9]

Following the much-discussed examples of whistleblowers such as Edward Snowden and Chelsea Manning, the received view of

---

[8] This definition of whistleblowing is mutuated from Ceva and Bocchiola (2018, 2019, 2020).

[9] Whistleblowing as a last resort is discussed, among others, by Jubb (1999, 15–16).

whistleblowing identifies it with unauthorized reports of some organizational wrongdoing, typically in the form of a leak to the media. Edward Snowden was a computer specialist working for the Central Intelligence Agency (CIA) first, and then a subcontractee for the National Security Agency (NSA). Snowden gained access to classified information concerning the global surveillance network through which the American secret services monitor telecommunication systems around the world. After trying unsuccessfully to share his qualms with some of his coworkers, Snowden flew out to Hong Kong, taking with him a great deal of classified information. He then leaked this information to journalists from the *Guardian* and the *Washington Post*. In June 2013, Snowden was charged with violating the 1917 Espionage Act and with theft of government property. Facing the possibility of lifetime imprisonment, he fled the country and currently lives in Russia, where President Putin has granted him temporary asylum.

Chelsea Manning was an American Marine who, while stationed in Iraq as an intelligence analyst, gained privileged access to classified information, some of which concerned crimes committed by U.S. troops. Manning leaked some 750,000 classified documents on such crimes to WikiLeaks; she was thus sentenced to thirty-five years of prison on a number of counts, including violation of the 1917 Espionage Act and theft of government property. After President Obama commuted her sentence, Manning was released from prison in May 2017.

Whistleblowers are often seen as individual advocates of justice and morality, who act conscientiously at the risk of their own personal safety. In this sense, whistleblowing appears to be an extraordinary conscientious act, akin to civil disobedience (see Boot 2017; Delmas 2015; Kumar and Santoro 2017). While some commentators view whistleblowing as a laudable, heroic act,[10] others insist on the risks this practice poses for the organizational

---

[10] Grant (2002) speaks of whistleblowers as "saints of a secular culture" (398).

culture. The main alleged risk is that whistleblowing may foster a culture of reciprocal suspicion among coworkers, which may end up violating their relations of trust as well as their rights to privacy. Moreover, when whistleblowing involves the disclosure of classified government information, it tends to be viewed as a threat to important general interests such as public security and criticized as a wrongful breach of a promissory obligation (see Boot 2017; Cole 2014; Sagar 2013). [11]

This view of whistleblowing as a conscientious act of contestation of some uses of office power can certainly capture what is at stake in many current occurrences of this practice. However, we also think that these cases do not cover the full spectrum of instances of whistleblowing, nor do they do justice to the structural role of this practice within a public ethics of office accountability. To determine this role, we embrace a different view of whistleblowing: We see it as an ordinary institutional practice of answerability that calls officeholders to answer for their conduct when a deficit of office accountability is suspected. From this point of view, whistleblowing must be institutionalized. In order to make officeholders reciprocally answerable for their conduct, external or internal reporting channels must be in place through which officeholders can discharge their duty to engage in answerability practices so that their responsibilities for political corruption can be established. [12] In the case of external whistleblowing, a report is made, for example, to the police or an anticorruption governmental body; when whistleblowing is internal, however, the report is typically addressed to a dedicated committee within the organization

---

[11] Along similar lines, Delmas (2015) discusses whistleblowing as an impermissible instance of vigilantism that threatens the rule of law.

[12] The emphasis on the communicative function of whistleblowing is important in differentiating our reading from an alternative self-centered view of this practice. In this alternative view, individual instances of whistleblowing could be presented as acts of personal disassociation with a corrupt practice and aimed at avoiding complicity with it so as to preserve the whistleblower's personal integrity (see Brenkert 2010; Davis 2003).

where the wrongdoing has occurred. The choice between internal or external channels for blowing the whistle depends on the kind of organizational wrongdoing and the organization in question. So, for example, unlawful uses of a power of office can be reported directly to the police. But when an employee starts to have growing doubts about the sources of funds provided by the private sector to finance a public project managed by her councillorship, it might be sensible that she first turn to the mayor's office. This internal reference is important from our point of view because it pinpoints officeholders' internal interrelated responsibilities for making their institution well-functioning by reacting to (actual or suspected) accountability deficits. We should also note that while internal reporting channels may be sufficient for large institutions, when smaller offices are involved, there might not be sufficient internal resources to make whistleblowing effective. Therefore, the availability of external reporting channels seems in order. Appropriately regulated whistleblowing must provide procedures suitable for such heterogeneous cases, thus assisting and unburdening the potential whistleblower.

This institutional take on whistleblowing as a lawful ordinary answerability practice can integrate the view of whistleblowing as an individual extraordinary and unauthorized extrema ratio (as was the case with Snowden and Manning). We think that the emphasis on the institutional dimension of whistleblowing is warranted in consideration of the crucial role that this practice has in calling officeholders to take up their anticorruption responsibilities in the face of an alleged office accountability deficit within their institution. Given their privileged position as "insiders," whistleblowers may disclose information that would otherwise be unavailable because it is either normally concealed or difficult to isolate. In this sense, whistleblowing contributes a great deal to identifying corrupt individual behavior as well as to understanding what may have gone wrong in a public institution. By blowing the whistle on alleged office accountability deficits, officeholders may initiate an internal investigative process for assigning retrospective individual and interrelated responsibilities among themselves. In this sense, whistleblowing is not exceptional, but rather an integral part of an institution's ability to establish answerability practices and for officeholders to fulfill their duty to engage in them, thus countering from the inside one of its major internal enemies.

Because blowing the whistle on alleged office accountability deficits is one of the ways in which officeholders may discharge their duty of answerability, to justify whistleblowing within a public ethics of office accountability is not only to say that it is permissible but, under certain conditions, obligatory. Engaging in answerability practices through whistleblowing requires the presence and accessibility of safe and effective reporting channels at the institutional level. The provisions required to this effect include removal of obstacles that may discourage individuals from coming forward through internal or external channels of whistleblowing, as appropriate. Admittedly, some of the disincentives to blowing the whistle are quite difficult to counteract because they also entail personal costs (e.g., jeopardizing a colleague's friendship). No institutional practice has the capacity to avoid these costs. In fact, evaluating the personal costs whistleblowers may face is largely a matter of personal ethics that (as happens with reference to many other issues of justice) falls outside the boundaries of a public ethics of office. Institutional action can, however—and it should—target professional costs, for example, by establishing such protective measures as safeguarding the confidentiality of the whistleblowers' revelations. Surely enough, whistleblowing protection should not be absolute, but it should also consider the impact whistleblowing may have on others' interests and rights (e.g., the collective interest in national security or the individual right to privacy). So, a careful investigation should follow any report, and officeholders must be made aware of the responsibilities associated with whistleblowing—for example, through establishing specific training programs at the workplace that go beyond formal legal measures.[13]

In summary, when officeholders engage in answerability practices facing alleged deficits of office accountability, one of the main challenges is to identify corrupt uses of powers of office, which are characteristic of elusive and often-hidden forms of officeholders' interactions. This identification is necessary in reconstructing what may have gone wrong in some institutional practice with respect to the institution's raison d'être (retrospective dimension). But urging that institutional action be taken to bring possible deficits of office accountability to light is just as important for consolidating a public ethics of office accountability (prospective dimension).

To be sure, whistleblowing is but one instance of the ways in which officeholders are called to discharge their duty to engage in answerability practices. Answerability may be implemented through various monitoring mechanisms, some of which may be routinized, while others may target specific institutional practices that are particularly susceptible to political corruption. In some European countries, such as Germany, for example, the majority of public institutions have implemented random controls of corruption-prone proceedings (Salvenmoser et al. 2010, 41–42). According to the recommendations of the German Federal Ministry of the Interior, when the federal administration is concerned, these controls should take the form of an internal audit. Internal audit units may be structured either centrally (at the level of the supreme federal authority) or peripherally (in the federal ministries and their executive agencies). The ministry executive

---

[13] These concerns are critical, for example, in two major initiatives designed to protect whistleblowers in the Netherlands (Whistleblowers Authority Act; see https://www.huisvoorklokkenluiders.nl/english) and the United Kingdom (Independent Office of the Whistleblower, see https://a02f9c2f-03a1-4206-859b-06ff2b21dd81.filesusr.com/ugd/88d04c_9754e54bc641443db902cd963687cb55.pdf).

decides on the structure of controls, taking into account the potential risks of corruption in specific cases. Based on the susceptibility to political corruption of a specific agency or some of its proceedings, the internal audit unit produces a catalogue of topics that it uses to plan an audit process. This audit plan must be presented to the agency executive for approval and covers the material, personnel, and scheduling aspects of the audit. Audits may have many forms; for example, they may be performed randomly, be required for specific reasons, or take the form of follow-up audits, with the aim of monitoring the implementation of earlier recommendations (German Federal Ministry of the Interior 2014). The official aim of these practices is to support officeholders in fulfilling their duties of office: "Internal audit units provide information and recommendations for administrative and technical supervision but is [sic] not a substitute for it. Staff should regard the internal audit unit as helping them carry out their duties" (German Federal Ministry of the Interior 2014, 61).

In this spirit, we can see how opposing political corruption requires following up on alleged accountability deficits (or the risk thereof) within a public institution. To oppose political corruption is irreducible to the censorship of some officeholder's corrupt behavior. Some positive actions are also necessary in order to uphold a public ethics of office accountability through institutional practices supportive of officeholders' conduct and their interrelated action.

5. Prospective anticorruption obligations

Finally, when a deficit of office accountability is confirmed, new anticorruption obligations are generated for officeholders. "Anticorruption" is how we label the responses to political corruption officeholders should give as an interrelated group of agents. This response must be tailored to counter the specific kind of wrong embodied by political corruption: a relational kind of wrong in the form of an interactive injustice. Therefore, the aim of an anticorruption strategy is to restore a just normative order of interactions. This aim cannot be solely pursued either by a third-party action (while this action can be useful to implement it) or by any one single officeholder in isolation (while an individual could initiate it). Because the inherent injustice of political corruption is a matter of the internal role-based relations between officeholders as they exercise their institutional functions, interactive justice can only be restored by officeholders' working interrelatedly. Officeholders' interrelated work is necessary to reestablish the normative order of interactions governed by office accountability that political corruption constitutively disrupts.

To see what it means and takes to establish anticorruption measures that can restore interactive justice by realizing office accountability, it is useful to reconsider cases of political corruption in public procurement tainted by bribery. As we have seen in Chapter 2, cases of political corruption in public procurement not only are frequent, but also display systemic features that make it hard to locate individual retrospective and contributive responsibilities. Typically, only some of the officeholders involved actually gain personally from a bribe. It is the very procedure of public procurement which is often vitiated and fails office accountability. What can be done to restore the interactive justice of institutional relations between the officeholders implicated in the corrupt practice?

As we have suggested, practices of answerability can bring about awareness of the failure of some officeholders to uphold office accountability. Investigation of such accountability deficits commonly reveals how certain institutional roles are "soft spots," in the sense of being more susceptible to corruption. For example, this is the case of contracting officials facing economically powerful and intimidating private contractors; but the same predicament arises for elected politicians whose agendas touch on the interests of such sectors as the pharmaceutical industry where influential lobbies operate. When an instance of political corruption materializes in some of these soft spots, anticorruption requires the correction of the deficit of office accountability thus verified. This correction may be pursued by adopting strategies for restoring just institutional relations. For example, think of the "four-eyes principle." This principle requires that two officeholders approve an institutional action before it can be implemented. In a refinement of the basic principle, a random rotation of authorized individuals serves as the second pair of eyes, so that no one knows in advance who exactly will be called on to vet a given decision.[14]

Further support for practices of officeholders' answerability may come from the digitalization of decision-making records. By facilitating access to relevant information from other institutional members, digitalized records may enhance officeholders' mutual answerability for their decision and render the decision-making process more readily open to internal (self)scrutiny. This practice may also promote the officeholders' commitment to office accountability by encouraging them to act in a way that, if asked, they could vindicate in good faith as coherent with the terms of their power mandate. The lack, "disappearance," or inaccessibility of documents is a typical feature of highly corrupt institutions. Information and communication technologies may contribute (significantly, albeit not definitively) to enhancing officeholders' answerability and thus to reducing the level of corruption, which is especially important in the areas of fiscal management and public procurement.[15]

We are not committed to recommending any of these particular strategies or, in fact, to providing a specific list of good practices against which officeholders can assess their institutional performance.[16] Our discussions have been illustrative of the kernel

---

[14] For a case study on the implementation of the "four eyes" in public procurement, see OECD 2015.

[15] For example, an e-Taxation and e-Procurement project of this kind has been activated in Croatia; see Council of Europe (2006).

[16] Best practices of self-assessment are, for example, core to the OECD *Public Integrity Maturity Models*. These models provide governments and public sector organizations with standards for making qualitative assessments of their integrity systems (OECD 2020). To the extent that such models are not just a way of grading institutions from the

of our normative approach to anticorruption. Notably, we have shown various ways in which anticorruption rests on a normative commitment to corroborating the mutuality of relations between officeholders and the interdependence of their uses of their powers of office in their institutional capacity. The efficacy of these strategies in particular institutional contexts can only be verified from "within," in consideration of the actual relations among specific officeholders. Nevertheless, we can make the general case that the rationale for implementing anticorruption practices should be informed by the restorative logic that we have thus far outlined. Insofar as the mandate of a certain power of office is the term of reference for vetting specific institutional decisions, we can see how anticorruption belongs to a public ethics of office accountability as we characterized it. Through practices of the kind we have discussed, no officeholder can be said to bear alone the responsibility of facing situations at high risk of corruption. By calling officeholders to partake in this new distribution of anticorruption responsibilities, answerability practices aim at restoring just institutional relations and enabling officeholders, in their interrelatedness, to (re)gain their position for fulfilling their duty of office accountability.

Our understanding of political corruption as a form of interactive injustice also has significant implications for the characterization of the state's responsibility to implement anticorruption measures by means of its coercive power. Because, as explained in Chapter 3, political corruption as a kind of interactive injustice is pro tanto inherently wrong, anticorruption measures of the kind we describe *ought* to be undertaken. Against some common wisdom, these measures may not be left entirely to a cost-benefit analysis. The core aspect of our argument is that the state is legitimated and required to use its coercive power to implement anticorruption

outside, according to some objective standards, they may also embody elements that help uphold office accountability.

measures because of the pro tanto wrongness of political corruption as a matter of interactive justice.

To be sure, as seen in Chapter 3, the normative assessment of political corruption should also consider the extent to which certain episodes are conducive to an enhancement of end-state justice in specific nonideal circumstances. This mitigated judgment may be warranted when political corruption produces some positive consequences that, notably, enhance the realization of individuals' subjective rights in nonideal conditions when the principles of end-state justice are disregarded. In these circumstances, for example, political corruption may serve as the "grease" that will ease a cumbersome bureaucratic machinery, which may undermine economic development by discouraging foreign financial investments in certain countries. By getting around such bureaucratic obstacles, the payment of bribes to local bureaucrats—even when it is done out of self-interest—may have the positive effect of allowing financial flows that end up enhancing the welfare of the local population. This consequentialist, distributive-justice-based evaluation has sometimes been interpreted to discount the wrongness of single instances of political corruption and to make the development of any anticorruption measures dependent on the outcome of a case-based cost-benefit analysis (see Nye 1967).

Of course, we recognize that the state is justified to act out of concern for the distributive inequalities caused by political corruption. For example, provisions may be enacted to contain the impact of political corruption on the most vulnerable sections of the population. Think of those policies of forced redistribution that have been developed to counteract the corruption of the judiciary. These policies are regarded as a remedy to the common condition that affluent citizens prevail in court litigation because they are in a position to bribe judges. However, the remedial efficacy of these initiatives is quite patchy and controversial. For example, certain studies have shown that actions aimed directly at redressing economic inequalities do not seem to be effective unless they are associated with other actions targeting specific corrupt relations. This is because in contexts where the corruption of judges is wide-spread, once the total income of less affluent citizens rises, they become corruptors too (see Begovic 2006). These observations may weaken the case for anticorruption so understood because of the inefficacy of these measures.

These end-state-justice, consequentialist observations notwith-standing, we have offered an argument to see how there is also a nonnegligible sense in which political corruption is interactively unjust and, therefore, anticorruption is presumptively necessary to restore interactive justice. There might be circumstances in which the development of anticorruption measures must also consider the other functions that the state must perform. This is the case with the scenario mentioned earlier, in which political corruption enhances distributive end-state justice. Should a conflict between different demands of justice occur, difficult trade-offs may prove to be necessary. But the institutional commitment to anticorruption matters even in these circumstances because it is grounded in a public ethics of office accountability, which is the normative pivot of institutional action.

To retrace our steps in this chapter, we can now see how the officeholders' duty of standing clear of political corruption is the direct reverse of their primary duty of office accountability. This explains the importance of recognizing that political corruption is itself an accountability deficit and, as such, a problem of public ethics in its own right. The officeholders' secondary duty to detect and assess deficits of office accountability by engaging in practices of answerability derives from the fact that institutional roles are oc-cupied by human beings, who are fallible. Therefore, officeholders should be aware that their behavior does not always respond ap-propriately to their duties of office. Practices of answerability are the way in which officeholders in interrelatedness try to diag-nose occurrences of political corruption in their institution. Such diagnoses are necessary to locate unjust relations and are, thus, the premises for finding remedies to them. Taking up anticorruption obligations is the way in which officeholders signal to each other their commitment to addressing the deficits of office accountability that underpin unjust institutional relations. And more practically, it is also the way officeholders can take interrelated action to restore an institutional environment that upholds office accountability and facilitates the fulfillment of their duty to stand clear of political corruption in the future.

6. Conclusion

In this chapter, contrary to some received views of anticorruption, we have shown why opposing political corruption should not be understood simply as a matter of promoting procedural remedies through stricter office regulations or through retributive measures such as punishing corrupt officeholders or removing them from office. Instead, because political corruption is a matter of officeholders' institutional conduct, we have argued that opposing political corruption requires a more "proactive" engagement of officeholders to restore just institutional relations as an instance of their commitment to a public ethics of office accountability. This means activating officeholders in their interrelatedness to fulfill their duty of office accountability and—when necessary—to adopt new strategies for realizing an institutional environment that can uphold the fulfillment of their duty.

The practice of holding officeholders answerable for the uses they make of their powers of office when they act in their institutional capacity requires that officeholders exercise those powers consciously and conscientiously. To hold officeholders retrospectively and prospectively answerable in this sense means to call them to take direct action to be vigilant when encountering deficits of office accountability. To appreciate how this practice is crucial for activating officeholders to engage in an ethics of office accountability, we have compared our proposal to the received approaches that aim to oppose political corruption by restricting the legal regulation of possible uses of powers of office. These approaches seek to counter political corruption by reducing officeholders' margins of discretion. We have shown why these approaches are unsatisfactory because they mean to diminish—rather than to enhance—the space for officeholders' reciprocally responsible use of their powers of office. Overregulation risks turning officeholders into overbureaucratized executors, rather than responsible agents capable of and committed to engaging one another with regard to their institutional conduct and interrelated work to keep their institution faithful to its raison d'être. Instead, the practice of answerability stresses that the duty to locate political corruption and find appropriate answers to it is mainly a task for the interrelated work of officeholders within an institution. When, thanks to the officeholders' engagement in practices of answerability, a deficit of office accountability is confirmed, officeholders acquire new, specific anticorruption obligations to restore the just normative order of interactions that political corruption constitutively disrupts.

This composite account shows how anticorruption is a component of a public ethics of office accountability binding on officeholders in both ideal and nonideal circumstances. However, to present anticorruption as a component of a public ethics of office accountability does not mean that it includes *any* measure taken to uphold such an ethics. Some measures are necessary to make officeholders vigilant of possible deficits of office accountability by engaging in daily practices of reciprocal answerability to make a public institution well-functioning. When something goes wrong and institutional action goes off track, anticorruption kicks in. In this sense, anticorruption is an internal strategy of institutional self-correction that is utilized when officeholders fail to act on their primary duty of office accountability.

Conclusion

The kernel of our engagement with political corruption— the corruption of public officials and institutions— has been to make political corruption an object of public ethics in its own terms. To understand political corruption in this way means to see a particular way in which it is an "internal enemy of public institutions." We developed this characterization in three steps.

In the first two chapters, we explained how the main source of political corruption is internal to a public institution. In Chapter 1, we described political corruption as a deficit of office accountability in the officeholders' interrelated conduct. Political corruption occurs anytime officeholders act in their institutional capacity but use their power of office to pursue an agenda whose rationale may not be vindicated as coherent with the terms of that power mandate.

The focus on office accountability sheds light on the difference that the officeholders' conduct makes for the quality of institutional practices, when individual officeholders use their powers of office as interrelated via their institutional roles. As we observed in Chapter 2, because institutional roles are structurally interrelated, the corrupt conduct of some officeholders may trigger institutional dynamics that can corrupt entire institutional practices. Political corruption is thus a property of public institutions that cease to be well-functioning, a dysfunction that undermines them from within. No public institution is immune to political corruption, no matter how well designed its formal rules, mechanism, and procedures may be. As an internal enemy, political corruption is a serious threat to the well-functioning of public institutions because

Political Corruption. Emanuela Ceva and Maria Paola Ferretti, Oxford University Press (2021). © Oxford University Press. DOI: 10.1093/oso/9780197567869.003.0007

officeholders' interrelated corrupt conduct can always make the institution fail its raison d'être.

This is the first analytical insight of our discussion. It sheds light on an important dimension of political corruption that has been overlooked in those institutionalist theories that point mainly at the external threats to, and negative influences on, an institution's integrity (e.g., financial infiltrations in electoral campaigns or partisan powers hijacking public decision making). Although such external sources of political corruption are serious, an exclusive focus on those sources risks missing the internal structural dimension of political corruption. Our analysis has shown that the major threats to the well-functioning of public institutions do come in fact from within those institutions. This kind of threat can never be ruled out by means of procedural regulatory interventions or reforms; it requires the officeholders' vigilant engagement to counterbalance the constant endogenous risk of failing their institution. This is why political corruption is the matter of a public ethics of office.

Explanation of the kind of threat political corruption poses to a public institution and why it is serious occupies the central normative chapter of the book. In Chapter 3, we argued that a fundamental kind of wrong of political corruption is internal to a public institution. Political corruption is inherently wrong from a moral point of view in a relational sense: It constitutes an interactive injustice. The way in which officeholders relate to each other in their institutional capacity should respond to a normative order that establishes a duty of office accountability. When officeholders exercise their powers of office in a corrupt manner, they violate their duty of office accountability; they thus alter ipso facto the normative order of their interactions and, ultimately, fail to treat each other as required by their normative status in that order. This failure reveals that political corruption (when it occurs within a legitimate or nearly just institutional setting) raises moral concerns of its own even in the absence of clearly identifiable negative consequences that may derive from it.

This is the second, normative insight of our discussion with respect to consequentialist assessments of political corruption, which concentrate only on its actual or foreseeable economic, legal, sociopolitical, or moral endogenous or exogenous implications. We have recognized the significance of these implications, but we have also argued that fully identifying the wrongness of political corruption with its negative consequences means to expose the normative assessment of this phenomenon to erratic and circumstantial causal considerations (whether certain negative consequences actually occur). To make political corruption itself— not just its consequences—an object of public ethics means to bring out the constitutive dimension of its wrongness. Moreover, by characterizing political corruption in terms of the moral relations between officeholders, we have pointed out how political corruption cannot be reduced to unlawful action or formal rule breaking. Focus on the relational dimension is crucial to showing clearly why officeholders ought not to act in a corrupt manner (even in the absence of formal prohibitions) and how they could stand clear of this risk.

Finally, the normative assessment of political corruption as a form of interactive injustice provided the basis for our argument that the principal resources for opposing political corruption should be internal to a public institution. In Chapter 4, we posited that whenever a deficit of office accountability is suspected, officeholders have a duty to engage in good faith in practices of answerability. These practices are aimed at establishing and assigning retrospective and prospective responsibilities for political corruption to officeholders, severally and as interrelated agents. This exercise is crucial to engage officeholders in a communicative practice, thus calling on them to respond to the threats that their allegedly corrupt conduct may pose to their institution's ability to remain faithful to its raison d'être. By engaging in this practice, officeholders can either rebut, in part or in full, or accept their implication in political corruption and also assume the prospective responsibility of sustaining the well-functioning of their institution in the future.

We argued that when, upon scrutinizing a possible deficit of office accountability, political corruption becomes manifest, new anticorruption obligations ensue for officeholders. In Chapter 5, we discussed anticorruption as the response officeholders should give to political corruption as an interrelated group of institutional role occupants. Anticorruption properly called thus designates the mechanisms of self-correction that a public institution should implement to restore a normative order of just interactions.

We can thus pinpoint the third insight of our discussion as concerns establishing the responsibilities for political corruption and for anticorruption. We have pointed to the importance of internalizing these practices by conceptualizing them as the components of a public ethics of office accountability capable of giving officeholders practical guidance for their institutional action. Conceiving of anticorruption as an integral component of an ethics of office accountability points to officeholders' responsibility to bring about a substantial change in the organizational environment of their institutions. This conception is an important complement and a corrective to current, mainly legalistic and regulatory, approaches to political corruption and anticorruption. These approaches consist mainly of top-down initiatives intended primarily to disincentivize corrupt behavior and punish corrupt officeholders. These approaches are partial because they only target certain instances of political corruption, such as cases of unlawful action or where the officeholders' relative causal responsibilities can be clearly assigned. In so doing, these approaches have a modest practical reach, because they fail to empower officeholders to bring about valuable change in their institutional environment.

Ultimately, our focus on political corruption as an internal enemy of public institutions calls on officeholders to oppose political corruption from the inside. By realizing office accountability in their institutional practices, officeholders can work together to make their institution well-functioning.

References

Amundsen, Inge. 1999. "Political Corruption: An Introduction to the Issues." Chr. Michelsen Institute Development Studies and Human Rights Working Paper 7: 1–32.

Anechiarico, Frank, and James B. Jacobs. 1996. *The Pursuit of Absolute Integrity: How Corruption Control Makes Government Ineffective*. Chicago: University of Chicago Press.

Ang, Yuen Yuen. 2020. *China's Gilded Age: The Paradox of Economic Boom and Vast Corruption*. Cambridge: Cambridge University Press.

Applbaum, Arthur. 1999. *Ethics for Adversaries. The Morality of Roles in Public and Professional Life*. Princeton, NJ: Princeton University Press.

Applbaum, Arthur. 1992. "Democratic Legitimacy and Official Discretion." *Philosophy and Public Affairs* 21 (3): 240–74.

Bagnoli, Carla. 2018. "Claiming Responsibility for Action under Duress." *Ethical Theory and Moral Practice*, 21 (4): 851–68.

Bagnoli, Carla, and Emanuela Ceva. Mimeo. "The Normative Source of Individual Responsibility under Systemic Corruption. A Coercion Based View."

Barber, Michael, Brandice Canes-Wrone, and Sharence Thrower. 2017. "Ideologically Sophisticated Donors: Which Candidates Do Individual Contributors Finance?" *American Journal of Political Science* 61 (2): 271–88.

Begovic, Boris. 2006. "Economic Inequality and Corruption." In *Third World Bank Conference on Inequality: Inequality, Politics and Power*. Washington, DC: World Bank. http://pdc.ceu.hu/archive/00003699/01/economic_inequality_and_corruption.pdf.

Bellamy, Richard. 2010. "Dirty Hands and Clean Gloves: Liberal Ideals and Real Politics." *European Journal of Political Theory* 9 (4): 412–30.

Bennett, Brian. 2020. "Inside Jared Kushner's Unusual White House Role." *Time*, January 16, 2020. https://time.com/5766186/jared-kushner-interview.

Boot, Eric. 2017. "Classified Public Whistleblowing: How to Justify a Pro Tanto Wrong." *Social Theory and Practice* 43 (3): 541–67.

Bovens, Mark. 2010. "Two Concepts of Accountability: Accountability as a Virtue and as a Mechanism." *Western European Politics* 33 (5): 946–67.

Bovens, Mark, Robert E. Goodin, and Thomas Schillemans, eds. 2014. *The Oxford Handbook of Public Accountability*. Oxford: Oxford University Press.

Bratman, Michael. 2013. *Shared Agency: A Planning Theory of Acting Together*. Oxford: Oxford University Press.

Brenkert, George G. 2010. "Whistle-blowing, moral integrity, and organizational ethics." In *Oxford Handbook of Business Ethics*, edited by George G. Brenkert, Tom L. Beauchamp, 563– 601. New York: Oxford University Press.

Brock, Gillian. 2018. "Varietà di Corruzione Politica: verso un resoconto più inclusivo." *Notizie di Politeia* 34 (129): 6–21.

Calhoum, Chesire. 1995. "Standing for Something." *Journal of Philosophy* 42 (5): 235–60.

Ceva, Emanuela. 2019. "Political Corruption as a Relational Injustice." *Social Philosophy and Policy* 35 (2): 118–37.

Ceva, Emanuela. 2016. *Interactive Justice*. New York: Routledge.

Ceva, Emanuela, and Michele Bocchiola. 2020. "Theories of Whistleblowing." *Philosophy Compass* 15 (1). doi.org/10.1111/phc3.12642 e12642.

Ceva, Emanuela, and Michele Bocchiola. 2019. "Personal Trust, Public Accountability, and the Justification of Whistleblowing." *Journal of Political Philosophy* 27 (2): 187–206.

Ceva, Emanuela, and Michele Bocchiola. 2018. *Is Whistleblowing a Duty?* Cambridge: Polity Press.

Ceva, Emanuela, and Maria Paola Ferretti. 2018. "Political Corruption, Individual Behaviour, and the Quality of Institutions." *Politics, Philosophy & Economics* 17 (2): 216–31.

Ceva, Emanuela, and Maria Paola Ferretti. 2017. "Political Corruption." *Philosophy Compass* 12 (12). doi.org/10-1111/phc3.12461.

Ceva, Emanuela, and Maria Paola Ferretti. 2014. "Liberal Democratic Institutions and the Damages of Political Corruption." *Les Ateliers de l'éthique/The Ethics Forum* 9 (1): 126–45.

Ceva, Emanuela, and Lubomira Radoilska. 2018. "Responsibility for Reason-Giving: The Case of Individual Tainted Reasoning in Systemic Corruption." *Ethical Theory and Moral Practice* 21 (4): 789–809.

Chiodelli, Francesco. 2019. "The Illicit Side of Urban Development: Corruption and Organised Crime in the Field of Urban Planning." *Urban Studies* 56 (8): 1611–17.

Chiodelli, Francesco, and Stefano Moroni. 2015. "Corruption in Land-Use Issues: A Crucial Challenge for Planning Theory and Practice." *Town Planning Review* 86 (4): 437–55.

Cohen, Gerry A. 2006. "Casting the First Stone: Who Can, and Who Can't, Condemn the Terrorists." *Royal Institute for Philosophy Supplement* 81 (58): 113–36.

Cole, David. 2014. "The Three Leakers and What to Do about Them." *New York Review of Books* 6. https://www.nybooks.com/articles/2014/02/06/three-leakers-and-what-do-about-them/.

Copp, David. 1997. "Defending the Principle of Alternate Possibilities: Blameworthiness and Moral Responsibility." *Nous* 31 (4): 441–66.

Council of Europe. 2006. *Anti-corruption Strategies and Action Plans in South-eastern Europe*, PC-TC(2006)16. https://rm.coe.int/16806ee7b6.

Darwall, Stephen. 2006. *The Second-Person Standpoint: Morality, Respect, and Accountability*. Cambridge, MA: Harvard University Press.

Davis, Michael. 2003. "Whistleblowing." In *Oxford Handbook of Practical Ethics*, edited by Hugh LaFollette, 539– 63. New York: Oxford University Press.

deLeon, Peter. 1993. *Thinking about Political Corruption*. Armonk, NY: M. E. Sharpe.

Della Porta, Donatella, and Alberto Vannucci. 2012. *The Hidden Order of Corruption. An Institutional Approach*. London: Routledge.

Della Porta, Donatella, and Alberto Vannucci. 2007. "Corruption and Anti-Corruption: The Political Defeat of 'Clean Hands' in Italy." *West European Politics* 30 (4): 830–53.

Delmas, Candice. 2015. "The Ethics of Government Whistleblowing." *Social Theory and Practice* 41 (1): 77–105.

De Wulf, Luc, and José B. Sokol. 2005. *Customs Modernization Handbook*. World Bank. https://siteresources.worldbank.org/intexpcomnet/resources/customs_modernization_handbook.pdf.

Duff, R. Anthony. 2018. "Responsibility and Reciprocity." *Ethical Theory and Moral Practice* 21 (4): 775–87.

Duff, R. Anthony. 2017. "Legal Punishment." In *Stanford Encyclopedia of Philosophy*, edited by Ed Zalta. https://plato.stanford.edu/entries/legal-punishment.

Ehrenfreund, Norbert. 2007. *The Nuremberg Legacy*. London: Palgrave Macmillan.

Emmet, Dorothy. 1966. *Rules, Roles and Relations*. London: Macmillan.

European Commission. 2017. *Updated Study on Corruption in the Healthcare Sector*. https://ec.europa.eu/home-affairs/sites/homeaffairs/files/20170928_study_on_healthcare_corruption_en.pdf.

Feinberg, Joel. 1970 a. "Collective Responsibility." *Journal of Philosophy* 65 (21): 674–88.

Feinberg, Joel. 1970 b. "The Expressive Function of Punishment." In *Doing and Deserving*, edited by J. Feinberg, 95–118. Princeton, NJ: Princeton University Press.

Feinberg, Joel. 1970 c. "The Nature and Value of Rights." *Journal of Value Inquiry* 4: 243–57.

Ferretti, Maria Paola. 2019. "A Taxonomy of Institutional Corruption." *Social Philosophy and Policy* 35 (2): 242–63.

French, Peter, ed. 1998. *Individual and Collective Responsibility*. Rochester, VT: Schenkman.

Friker, Miranda. 2016. "What's the Point of Blame? A Paradigm Based Explanation." *Nous* 50 (1): 165–83.

German Federal Ministry of the Interior. 2014. *Integrity Rules*. https://www.bmi.bund.de/SharedDocs/downloads/EN/publikationen/2014/rules-on-integrity.pdf?__blob=publicationFile.

Gilbert, Margaret. 2000. *Sociality and Responsibility*. Lanham, MD: Rowman and Littlefield.

Grant, Colin. 2002. "Whistle Blowers: Saints of Secular Culture." *Journal of Business Ethics* 39 (4): 391–99.

Guala, Francesco. 2016. *Understanding Institutions*. Princeton, NJ: Princeton University Press.

Hart, H. L. A. 1968. *Punishment and Responsibility. Essays in the Philosophy of Law*. Oxford: Oxford University Press.

Hart, H. L. A. 1955. "Are They Natural Rights?" *The Philosophical Review* 64 (2): 175–91.

Heywood, Paul, ed. 2015. *The Routledge Handbook of Political Corruption*. London: Routledge.

Hooker, Brad. 2015. "Rule Consequentialism." In *The Stanford Encyclopedia of Philosophy*, edited by Ed Zalta. https://plato.stanford.edu/entries/consequentialism-rule/#OldObjRulCon.

Jain, Arvind K. 2001. "Corruption: A Review." *Journal of Economic Surveys* 15 (1): 71–121.

Jennings, Bruce. 1995. "Legislative Ethics and Moral Minimalism." In *Representation and Responsibility: Exploring Legislative Ethics*, edited by Bruce Jennings and Daniel Callahan, 149–66. New York: Plenum Press.

Johnston, Michael. 2005. *Syndromes of Corruption*. Cambridge: Cambridge University Press.

Jubb, Peter B. 1999. "Whistleblowing: A Restrictive Definition and Interpretation." *Journal of Business Ethics* 21: 77–94.

Keneally, Megan, and John Santucci. 2017. "Ivanka Trump Taking Formal Role in Administration amid Ethics Concerns." ABC News, March 29. https://abcnews.go.com/Politics/ivanka-trump-taking-formal-role-administration/story?id=46454858.

Knights, Mark. 2018. "Explaining. Away: Corruption in Pre-modern Britain." *Social Philosophy and Policy* 35 (2): 94–117.

Knights, Mark. 2014. "Samuel Pepys and Corruption." *Parliamentary History* 33 (1): 19–35.

Klockars, Carl B. 1980. "The Dirty Harry Problem." *Annals of the American Academy of Political and Social Science* 452: 33–47.

Klosko, George. 1992. *The Principle of Fairness and Political Obligation*. London: Rowman and Littlefield.

Kodi, M. 2008. *Transition and Governance in the DRC during the Transition Period. (2003–6)*. ISS Monograph Series. https://issafrica.s3.amazonaws.com/site/uploads/mono148fullback.pdf.

Kolstad, Ivar. 2012. "Corruption as Violation of Distributed Ethical Obligations." *Journal of Global Ethics* 8 (2–3): 239–50.

Korsgaard, Christine M. 1996. *The Sources of Normativity*. Cambridge: Cambridge University Press.

Kumar, Manohar, and Daniele Santoro. 2017. "A Justification of Whistleblowing." *Philosophy and Social Criticism* 43 (1): 669–84.

Kurer, Oskar. 2005. "Corruption: An Alternative Approach to Its Definition and Measurement." *Political Studies* 53 (1): 222–39.

La Palombara, Joseph. 1994. "Structural and Institutional Aspects of Corruption." *Social Research* 61 (2): 325–50.

Lambsdorff, Johann Graf. 2009. "The Organisation of Anticorruption: Getting the Incentives Right." In *Corruption, Global Security, and World Order*, edited by Robert Rotberg, 389–415. Baltimore, MD: Brookings Institution Press.

Le Billon, Philippe. 2003. "Buying Peace or Fuelling War: The Role of Corruption in Armed Conflicts." *Journal of International Development* 15 (4): 413–26.

Lessig, Lawrence. 2018. *America, Compromised*. Chicago: University of Chicago Press.

Lessig, Lawrence. 2014. "What an Originalist Would Understand 'Corruption' to Mean." *California Law Review* 102 (1): 1–24.

Lessig, Lawrence. 2013. "Institutional Corruption Defined." *Journal of Law and Medical Ethics* 41 (3): 553–55.

Lessig, Lawrence. 2011. *Republic Lost: How Money Corrupts Congress—and a Plan to Stop It*. Boston: Hachette.

List, Christian, and Philip Pettit. 2011. *Group Agency: The Possibility, Design, and Status of Corporate Agents*. Oxford: Oxford University Press.

Luban, David. 2012. "The Publicity Principle." In *The Theory of Institutional Design*, edited by Robert E. Goodin, 154–98. Cambridge: Cambridge University Press.

Marks, Jonathan H. 2013. "What's the Big Deal?: The Ethics of Public-Private Partnerships Related to Food and Health." Edmond J. Safra Working Paper 11. https://ssrn.com/abstract=2268079.

May, Larry. 1992. *Sharing Responsibility*. Chicago: University of Chicago Press.

May, Larry. 1997. *The Morality of Groups*. Notre Dame, IN: University of Notre Dame Press.

Mellema, Gregory. 2016. *Complicity and Moral Accountability*. Notre Dame, IN: University of Notre Dame Press.

Mendus, Susan. 2009. *Politics and Morality*. Cambridge: Polity Press.

Mill, John Stuart. 1963–91. *The Collected Works of John Stuart Mill*, edited by John M. Robson. Toronto: University of Toronto Press.

Miller, David. 2017. "Justice." In *The Stanford Encyclopedia of Philosophy*, edited by Edward Zalta. https://plato.stanford.edu/entries/justice/ #RelaVsNonRelaJust.

Miller, Seumas. 2018. "Corruption." In *The Stanford Encyclopedia of Philosophy*, edited by Edward Zalta. https://plato.stanford.edu/archives/win2018/entries/corruption.

Miller, Seumas. 2017. *Institutional Corruption. A Study in Applied Philosophy*. Cambridge: Cambridge University Press.

Miller, Seumas. 2014. "Social Institutions." In *The Stanford Encyclopedia of Philosophy*, edited by Edward Zalta. https://plato.stanford.edu/archives/win2014/entries/social-institutions.

Miller, Seumas, Peter Roberts, and Edward Spence. 2005. *Corruption and Anti-Corruption. An Applied Philosophical Approach*. Upper Saddle River, NJ: Pearson.

Mokrosinska, Dorota. 2012. *Rethinking Political Obligation: Moral Principles, Communal Ties, Citizenship*. New York: Palgrave.

Mokrosinska, Dorota. 2018. "The People's Right to Know and State Secrecy." *Canadian Journal of Law and Jurisprudence* 31 (1): 87–106.

Murphy, Coleen. 2017. *The Conceptual Foundations of Transitional Justice*. New York: Cambridge University Press.

Nye, Joseph. S. 1967. "Corruption and Political Development: A Cost-Benefit Analysis." *American Political Science Review* 61 (82): 417–27.

O'Neill, Onora. 2006. "Transparency and the Ethics of Communication." In *Transparency: The Key to Better Governance*, edited by Christopher Hood and David Heald, 79–90. Oxford: Oxford University Press.

Oppenheim, Maya. 2017. "Ivanka Trump New White House Job Not Nepotism Because She Isn't Being Paid, Says Donald Trump Surrogate." *Independent*, March 31. https://www.independent.co.uk/news/world/americas/ivanka-trump-white-house-job-not-nepotism-paid-west-wing-office-donald-trump-surrogate-jason-miller-a7659586.html.

Organisation for Economic Cooperation and Development. 2020. *OECD Public Integrity Handbook*. Paris: OECD Publishing. doi.org/10.1787/ac8ed8e8-en.

Organisation for Economic Cooperation and Development. 2015. *Effective Delivery of Large Infrastructure Projects: The Case of the New International Airport of Mexico City*. Paris: OECD Publishing.

Parker, Ashley, and Philip Rucker. 2018. "Where Is Ivanka? First Daughter Seeks Control in Dual Role as White House Aide." *The Washington Post*, March 12, 2018. https://www.denverpost.com/2018/03/12/ivanka-trump-role-white-house.

Philp, Mark. 2015. "The Definition of Political Corruption." In *The Routledge Handbook of Political Corruption*, edited by Paul Heyward, 42–56. London: Routledge.

Philp, Mark. 2001. "Access, Accountability and Authority: Corruption and the Democratic Process." *Crime, Law and Social Change* 36 (4): 357–77.

Philp, Mark. 1997. "Defining Political Corruption." *Political Studies* 45 (3): 436–62.

Philp, Mark, and Elizabeth Dávid-Barrett. 2017. "Realism about Political Corruption." *Annual Review of Political Science* 18: 387–402.

Radder, Hans, ed. 2010. *The Commodification of Academic Research*. Pittsburgh: University of Pittsburgh Press.

Rawls, John. 1971. *A Theory of Justice*. Cambridge, MA: Harvard University Press.

Reuters. 2013. "World Bank President Calls Corruption 'Public Enemy No. 1.'" December 19. https://www.reuters.com/article/us-worldbank-corruption-idUSBRE9BI11P20131219.

Ripstein, Arthur. 2009. *Force and Freedom: Kant's Legal and Political Philosophy*. Cambridge, MA: Harvard University Press.

Robertson, Elizabeth, Laura Atherton, and Dylan G. Moses. 2015. *Biggest Risk of Corruption in the Construction Industry. The Global Picture*. http://www.klgates.com/files/Publication/e3e0dfee-dc39–4ab8–8c4e-14fbabd10c4e/Presentation/PublicationAttachment/36557fb6–891f-4020-aadd-209aa092c330/Biggest_Risk_of_Corruption_in_the_Construction_Industry_Whitepaper.pdf.

Rodwin, Marc A. 2013. "Institutional Corruption and the Pharmaceutical Industry." Special Issue of the *Journal of Law, Medicine and Ethics* 41 (3): 544–746.

Rose-Ackerman, Susan. 1999. *Corruption and Government: Causes, Consequences, and Reforms*. Cambridge: Cambridge University Press.

Rose-Akerman, Susan. 1975. "The Economics of Corruption." *Public Economics* 4: 187–203.

Rothstein, Bo, and Jan Teorell. 2008. "What Is Quality of Government: A Theory of Impartial Political Institutions." *Governance* 21 (2): 165–90.

Rothstein, Bo, and Aiysha Varraich. 2017. *Making Sense of Corruption*. Cambridge: Cambridge University Press.

Sagar, Rahul. 2013. *Secrets and Leaks. The Dilemma of State Secrecy*. Princeton, NJ: Princeton University Press.

Salvenmoser, Steffen, Frank Weise, Rainer Heck, Kai-D. Bussmann, and Andreas Schroth. 2010. *Kriminalität im öffentlichen Sektor* Frankfurt am Main: Pricewaterhouse Coopers.

Sandel, Michael. 2013. *What Money Can't Buy: The Moral Limits of Markets*. New York: Penguin.

Sberna, Salvatore, and Alberto Vannucci. 2013. "'It's the Politics, Stupid!'. The Politicization of Anti-Corruption in Italy." *Crime, Law and Social Change* 60 (5): 565–93.

Sher, George. 2006. *In Praise of Blame*. New York: Oxford University Press.

Simmons, John. 1979. *Moral Principles and Political Obligations*. Princeton: Princeton University Press.

Somers, Mark John. 2001. "Ethical Codes of Conduct and Organizational Context: A Study of the Relationship between Codes of Conduct, Employee Behaviour and Organizational Values." *Journal of Business Ethics* 30: 185–95.

Sparling, Robert. 2019. *Political Corruption: The Underside of Civic Morality.* Philadelphia: University of Pennsylvania Press.

Sparling, Robert. 2017. "Impartiality and the Definition of Corruption." *Political Studies* 66 (2): 376–91.

Sparling, Robert. 2014. "Le Prince et le problème de la corruption: réflexions sur une aporie machiavélienne." ' *Les ateliers de l'éthique / Ethics Forum* 9: 8–27.

Stark, Andrew. 1997. "Beyond Quid Pro Quo: What Is Wrong with Private Gain from Public Office." *American Political Science Review* 91 (1): 108–11.

Thompson, Dennis. 2018. "Theories of Institutional Corruption." *Annual Review of Political Science* 21 (26): 1–19.

Thompson, Dennis. 2013. "Two Concepts of Corruption." Edmond J. Safra Research Lab, Working Papers 16.

Thompson, Dennis. 2005. "Two Concepts of Corruption: Making Electoral Campaigns Safe for Democracy." *George Washington Law Review* 73 (12): 1036–69.

Thompson, Dennis. 1995. *Ethics in Congress: From Individual to Institutional Corruption.* Washington, DC: Brookings Institution.

Thompson, Dennis. 1993. "Mediated Corruption: The Case of the Keating Five." *American Political Science Review* 87 (2): 369–81.

Thompson, Dennis. 1980. "Moral Responsibility of Public Officials: The Problem of Many Hands." *American Political Science Review* 74 (4): 905–16.

Transparency International. 2016. *Corruption Perception Index 2016.* https://issuu.com/transparencyinternational/docs/2016_cpireport_en.

Transparency International. 2004. *Global Corruption Report.* London: Pluto Press.

United Nations Development Program (UNDP). 2010. "Fighting Corruption in Post-Conflict and Recovery Situations. Learning from the Past." http://contentext.undp.org/aplaws_publications/2594849/Fighting%20corruption%20in%20post-conflict%20and%20recovery%20situations.pdf.

Uslaner, Eric M. 2015. "The Consequences of Corruption." In *Routledge Handbook of Political Corruption,* edited by Paul M. Heywood, 199–211. London: Routledge.

Vallentyne, Peter. 1988. "Teleology, Consequentialism, and the Past." *The Journal of Value Inquiry* 22 (2): 89–101.

Waldron, Jeremy. 2003. "The Primacy of Justice." *Legal Theory* 9 (4): 269–64.

Waller, Bruce. 2011. *Against Moral Responsibility.* Cambridge, MA: MIT Press.

Walzer, Michael. 1973. "Political Action: The Problem of Dirty Hands." *Philosophy and Public Affairs* 2 (2): 160–80.

Warren, Mark E. 2006. "Political Corruption as Duplicitous Exclusion." *Political Science and Politics* 39 (4): 803–807.

Warren, Mark E. 2004. "What Does Corruption Mean in a Democracy." *American Journal of Political Science* 48 (2): 328–43.

Watson, Gary. 2004. "Two Faces of Responsibility." In *Agency and Answerability: Selected Essays*, edited by G. Watson, 260–88. Oxford: Oxford University Press.

Weinstock, Daniel. 2019. "Corruption in Adversarial System: The Case of Democracy." *Social Philosophy and Policy* 35 (2): 212–41.

Williams, Bernard. 1995. "Internal Reasons and the Obscurity of Blame." In *Making Sense of Humanity and Other Philosophical Papers*, edited by Bernard Williams, 40–43. Cambridge: Cambridge University Press.

Winston, Kenneth. 1999. "Constructing Law's Mandate." In *Recrafting the Rule of Law: The Limits of Legal Order*, edited by David Dyzenhaus, 283–308. Portland, OR: Hart Publishing.

Wolf, Susan. 1990. *Freedom within Reason*. New York: Oxford University Press.

Young, Iris Marion. 1990. *Justice and the Politics of Difference*. Princeton, NJ: Princeton University Press.

Zacka, Bernardo. 2017. *When the State Meets the Street*. Cambridge, MA: Harvard University Press.

Zimmerman, Michael J. 1988. *An Essay on Moral Responsibility*, Totowa, NJ: Rowman and Littlefield.

Index

For the benefit of digital users, indexed terms that span two pages (e.g., 52–53) may, on occasion, appear on only one of those pages.